INTRO

By Emilia Korczynska,

True to form - *hey Folks!* You know you've overdosed PLG when you stab your toe on your nightly commute to the bathroom and the first thing that comes to your mind is *"bad UX!!!"*. But on a more serious note - that's the case with most SaaS products still, in 2023. My job inevitably forces me to test a lot of martech tools - and seeing the same common mistakes that have a huge negative impact on user experience, activation - and thus - retention - over and over again - is a real pain in the...big toe. Or - as we say in Poland - *"it makes the potatoes in my basement rot"*. From merciless 20-step product tours without the "X" button, to no self-serve support in-app altogether - I've seen it all.

So when I joined Userpilot on a cloudy morning in January 2020 and took over the company newsletter - it quickly turned into what one of the subscribers later aptly dubbed "Product Rants". Three and a half years later, I've produced enough Product Rantz to peek into every dark corner of User Experience. And at that point - we've decided to pull all the teardowns together into a value-packed, and South Park-style-humor-laden manual - that you're now holding in your hands.

Some of you may think I'm a negative Nancy - but I do believe that PLG lessons wrapped in stories from personal experience stick a lot better than dry theory and stickiness is what we're all after here, aren't we? So within this book - you will find best practices (and worst practices!), actionable tips, insights and examples on several Product-Led Growth topics.
Enjoy and drop a line at **emilia@userpilot.co**!

By Yazan Sehwail, Userpilot co-founder & CEO

In today's world of SaaS and cloud-based B2B enterprise software, the customer journey has shifted entirely into the product itself. From the initial free trial to activation, adoption, retention, and expansion revenue, the product experience has become the center of growth for many companies.

However, the complexity and richness of features in B2B software can often lead to a significant portion of those features being underutilized, costing companies billions of dollars in lost R&D and missed upsell opportunities.

Enter the product experience era, where it is no longer enough for product teams to simply build and design the best features. Instead, the product as a whole must be personalized and tailored to the individual user persona and stage of the user journey.

By facilitating the adoption of different features at the appropriate times, the product can drive growth through activation, retention, and expansion.

But how do product teams navigate this new landscape and ensure that their products are driving growth and success? That is the question we aim to answer in this book, exploring the latest trends and strategies in the product experience era.

TABLE OF CONTENTS

USER ACTIVATION
Definition

We realized that there is a lot of misunderstanding between the 'AHA!' moment and user activation.

A lot of people think that the 'AHA!' moment and user activation are the same, but they actually happen at separate times.

The 'AHA!' moment is just a mental state when your users perceive the value you're offering and think:

"Wow, this is amazing. I think I'm starting to like this tool!".

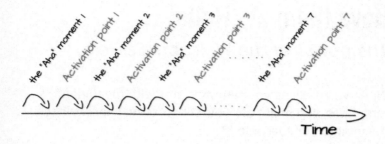

User activation is actually the moment when your users get value. It's a phase where a user fully engages or activates the initial set of persona-relevant key features in the product.

As one of the most important steps on the User Journey and one of the five Pirate Metrics, you need to define what counts as Activation for your product.

Your SaaS's Activation Rate then is the percentage of users who get to that key event – and often, optimizing your Activation Rate has the greatest downstream impact on the revenue of any KPI you should be tracking.

Have them at "Hello"
The power of the Welcome Screen

When you're filling your empty states with meaningful templates, you might ask yourself "how do I know what's meaningful for each user"?

Welcome screens are mostly seen as an optional pleasantry in SaaS. According to our State of SaaS Onboarding 2020 research (watch this space! New edition is coming!) the Welcome Screen is the most underutilized piece of real estate in SaaS. 40% of SaaS companies don't use them at all, and the majority of those who do only use them to greet their new users. Big mistake!

If used right, a Welcome Screen can:

1) Help you segment your new users by role, goals, and use case. All you need is a microsurvey. This, in turn, can be critical for personalizing their onboarding experience. And as we all know – the more personalized and relevant the onboarding flow, the faster your users understand the value of your product.

Just look at this example from ConvertKit:

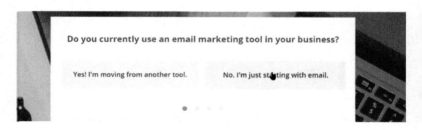

Your answer to this question will determine the further onboarding flow you see. (Red pill, blue pill from 'The Matrix').
- Obviously, if you're moving from another email marketing tool, you probably have an email list that you want to import.
- You will also be more familiar with email marketing in general – so Convertkit can skip some of the basic explanations for you.
- On the other hand – if you're a complete newbie – you may need help with basic things - like collecting your first subscribers or sending your first email.

Asking the right question in the Welcome Screen is critical for how relevant your onboarding is, and for your Time To Value.

2) Microsurveys in Welcome Screens can also be used to reduce the friction for invited users from company accounts. They often miss the new user onboarding and are left to their own devices once they've accepted the invite. Here's an example of a microsurvey that can be used to learn about their goal, and to guide them on how to achieve it + how to build it in Userpilot:

3) Finally, there are the referred users.

If your product is inherently viral, and your existing users invite other users or share links to certain parts of your platform: the Welcome Screen becomes an invaluable marketing asset. You can literally use it to sell your referred user on the idea of joining your platform/ network/ marketplace.

Here's an example of a Welcome Screen built in Userpilot for an app with a viral coefficient:

Welcome {{name}}!

Emilia is inviting you to join her backlink building partnership!

BacklinkManager allows Emilia to build more backlinks faster and more efficiently than Google Sheets. You can view Emilia's sheet without signing up - but honestly - why would you miss such opportunity? 😊

It's easy and it's free!

REGISTER (recommended)

...OR CONTINUE AS A GUEST

To sum up:

- Use the Welcome Screen to elicit the role and goal of users
- Personalize the follow-up onboarding flows accordingly
- Use a different Welcome Screen for invited users
- Use Welcome Screens to market your product to new leads from referrals

No IKEA, not my big day tomorrow
Personalization done wrong = cringe

One day, I received an email from IKEA saying, 'Emilia, it's your big day tomorrow!'

No, it's not 'my big day' tomorrow, IKEA. Thanks for the reminder about your transport, but it's not like I'm going to celebrate the anniversary of the arrival of your BRIMNES wardrobe with cake and champagne every year from now on. Did this attempt at personalization make me love IKEA more? Nej, not really. While I love IKEA for many reasons, this email made it sound like a flat-pack of emotion, the Volvo of romantic feelings to me.

Many B2B SaaS businesses have jumped on the 'personalization' bandwagon as well. Unfortunately, most think personalization is about throwing in the first name tag in the confirmation email and welcome screen. Or about calling me a 'friend' in their email subject line and faking familiarity. **In my experience, most SaaS companies get personalization completely wrong**, thus passing on the opportunity to leverage it to increase activation, conversion, and retention.

Why do companies get personalization wrong?

First, they confuse "personal" with "proper", and "trendy" with "timely". They fake familiarity where it's actually not proper. When in real life would you call a complete stranger you're trying to sell something to "a friend"?

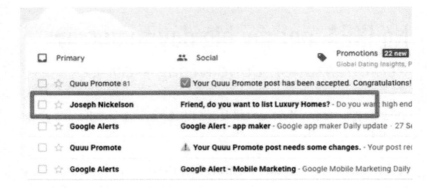

Source: hyperise

Imagine cashiers in supermarkets or managers in restaurants calling you a friend. That would be plain creepy in real life, right? Then why do we insist on doing it online?

No, faking familiarity, or overusing Bernie Sanders memes to look cool won't earn you your customer's respect (and their business).

What will?

- Personalizing your user's onboarding experience to their use case to help them get their job done faster.
- Following up diligently through email to see if your product solved their problem.

This is the kind of personalization that shows you really care - while failing at the FIRSTNAME tag - points to the exact opposite. Companies should only personalize when they have some kind of personal interaction with the customer - and to the extent they had it.

Now, why do companies fail at using personalization right?

Well, many don't understand what personalization means. Since we have (hopefully) got that one out of the way: there's another reason. **Product analytics tools are notoriously difficult to read.**

As a result, few SaaS companies actually know which touchpoints each user persona has with their company and their product. And hence - they don't know how to personalize their in-app experiences at these touchpoints.
This, in turn, means a lot of SaaS companies focus on superficial demographic data while creating their 'user persona avatars' - think 'Marketing Mary' or 'Manager Tom'.

As Louis Grenier from EveryoneHatesMarketers points out: People buy your SaaS product to get a specific job done (think JTBD framework), not because they've got two kids and love the color red.

Louis Grenier · 1st   ···
I fight marketing bullshit with radical differentiation: EveryoneHatesMar...
1d · 🌐

You NEVER buy something because you're between 20 and 30, because you are an HR professional, or because you have 2 Cavalier King Charles spaniel dogs.

You buy to get a job done.

And sometimes this job is mostly done by people in their 20s, by HR pros, or by folks who own super expensive dogs.

#marketing #psychology

🔵 💬 👍 131 · 28 comments

Source: Louis Grenier

How to personalize right in your SaaS

As you may have guessed - the **right way to personalize in SaaS is by**:

a) segmenting your users by their Jobs-To-Be-Done;
b) helping them get their jobs done ASAP.

ConvertKit, an email marketing tool for creatives, makes sure their new users get what they want ASAP.

By asking them what they want to accomplish in the welcome screen (remember the example from earlier)?

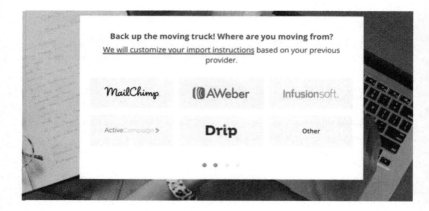

If you choose you're moving from a specific tool, they will give you a few options and then customize your moving instructions to help you get that done faster.

To sum up:

1. Decide what common jobs your users 'hire' your product for;

2. Create a microsurvey with these jobs as options in your welcome screen (you can create them code-free using Userpilot).

3. Tailor the onboarding experiences accordingly - show your users' the shortest path to achieving their goal, one at a time.

They will thank you.

Want higher activation?
Swipe right on gamification.
Swipe left on empty states.

Gamify your onboarding in 4 steps

Did you know, a third of your new users will leave without even trying your product? Why? Because of 'fear of the white canvas'.

If the first thing your new users see when they sign up for an app is an empty dashboard, a lot of them will give up before they have even started. Empty states are like an empty dance floor at a party, no one knows how to make the first move. So how do you reduce the cognitive load associated with figuring out how to use a new tool? Fill that empty state with a meaningful template relevant to the users' use case.

Shiv Patel, a founder of Autopilot, a marketing automation tool, used his experience from working as a Product Manager at WeWork to figure it out. Much like potential new members didn't see the point of a shared co-working space until they saw the events and networking opportunities at meetups, the new users of his marketing tool didn't get the value of the product until they saw some ready-made workflows.

So Shiv took the templates out of the app and let the user peruse them and play with them before even leaving their email address. That way - once they did sign up, they already had something to start from. This reduced the Time To Value massively and doubled Autopilot's activation rates.

But what to show your new users? As mentioned before, welcome screens are a great way to learn about them. Before you pull out that lengthy survey though, there's a great alternative: gamify the whole onboarding experience, starting from the welcome screen:

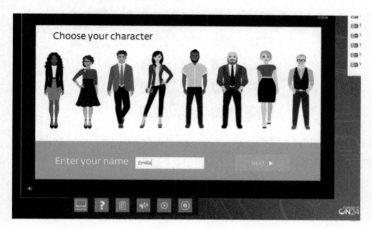

I was recently taking a cyber security training and I saw this example of gamification. Why don't we all ask our users to pick their avatars and game scenarios, so we can find out about their roles and use cases in a fun, non-intrusive way?

And later on:
- Add onboarding checklists with tasks related to activation points, and financial incentives for completing each one:

- Create badges to reward reaching higher proficiency levels (like Hubspot) or completing advanced checklists:

- Use leaderboards to encourage rivalry between users of company accounts...

These are all gamification elements that make onboarding more fun - and increase the chance for new user activation.

According to our recent survey: only 20% of SaaS companies use gamification in their onboarding. Wouldn't you want to be one of the trailblazers?

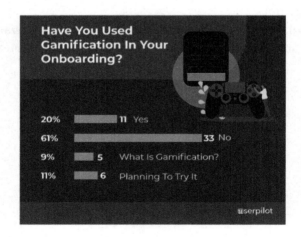

There's no valid benchmark for this crucial metric ⊖
And it has the largest impact on your MRR

I'm always harping about this, but I was just putting this presentation together for the SaaS Metrics Summit and it struck me again: **Activation (the moment when your user actually gets the core benefit of your product) has the biggest impact on revenue** from all the Pirate Metrics.

Metric	MRR increase after 12 months if metric increases 25%
Acquisition	25%
Activation	34%
Revenue	25%
Retention	31.07%
Referrals	7.44%

If a 25% increase in activation contributes to a 34% increase in MRR in 12 months, activation affects MRR by the factor of x1.34 - compared to x1 for acquisition and x0.3 for referrals.

So wouldn't it be great to be able to consistently measure it, compare it to benchmarks, and use some tried-and-tested playbooks to improve it? Ha, I wish.

Measuring this elusive metric causes SaaS companies so much trouble in itself. Not to mention the definition of 'Activation' varies not only from product to product, but also from persona to persona and use cases. So how can you possibly compare it between different companies? It would be like comparing apples to oranges.

My former colleague, Aazar Shad, even tried - out of sheer curiosity - to ask SaaS companies about their activation rate. The distribution of the answers so far was far from normal...A lot of the businesses didn't even track the metric at all! And I can't blame them.

What's is your current user activation rate (on average)?

21 out of 22 people answered this question

19.0%	15-20%	4 responses
19.0%	46-55%	4 responses
9.5%	11-14%	2 responses
9.5%	26-30%	2 responses
9.5%	31-35%	2 responses
9.5%	36-45%	2 responses
9.5%	4-6%	2 responses
9.5%	71-80%	2 responses
4.8%	0-3%	1 response
0.0%	21-25%	0 responses
0.0%	56-70%	0 responses
0.0%	6-10%	0 responses
0.0%	81-90%	0 responses

Even at Userpilot (I daresay, as a platform with solid product analytics, measuring things is our forte) we had a bit of a conundrum recently on what our free trial user activation point really was.

Traditionally, we assumed that an activated user is one that has performed the following activation events:

1. Installed the javascript code in their app
2. Created at least one experience flow

...but when we actually sat down to look at the real data of the new users from our free trial (in an attempt to check if the users from self-serve trial signup or the demo had a higher activation rate) the data threw us off:

- there were a whole lot of users who installed the js code and had several web sessions looking at the analytics, but didn't build any experiences...

- then there were users who built several experiences, and had a number of web sessions but have not installed the js code (meaning they couldn't access their user analytics or deploy the experiences to their app).

Both groups could actually get value from the product at this point...This illustrates how careful you need to be in deciding what actually counts as activation for you. Having said that - should you just throw your hands up in the air in despair? No! It may sound like a motivational-guru mantra but... you just shouldn't compare yourself to others. You should compare yourself (now) to yourself (yesterday). While you can't effectively say how you compare to an 'industry standard' (because there is no standard) you can still measure and improve from your own benchmark.

How do you define + measure activation?

First, you need to know what in-app events need to happen for a specific persona to get their job done in your product.

Then, you count how many people have performed these in-app events in a specific period of time, and divide it by all the new users within the particular person in that time period.

Why is it important to keep different personas apart?

Let me give you an example: If you have an email marketing tool, you may get several types of users who come to your tool with different Jobs-To-Be-Done. Let's take two of them:

1. A blogger who is just starting out and wants to use your tool to collect subscribers on their blog;
2. An e-commerce store owner who is switching from another tool, and has a list of 10,000 subscibers already.

For the first persona, the key activation events will be:
1. Creating their first signup form
2. Embedding it on their blog
3. Collecting their first subscribers

For the second persona, the events will be:
1. Uploading their email list
2. Creating their first newsletter
3. Sending their first newsletter to their email list

That's why ConvertKit (from the examples earlier) actually asks its users if they have used another tool before.

Now, how to improve activation metrics?

Know your user persona and their JTBD well.

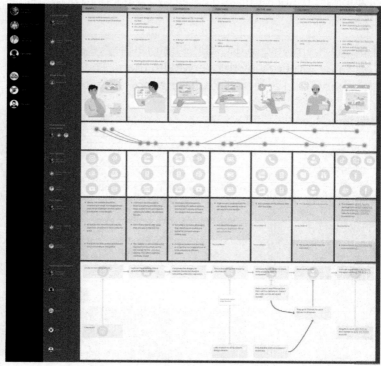

Source: UXpressia

In order to improve your activation rate, you first need to define activation. To do that, you need to actually understand your persona and the different jobs they have that need to be done in your tool.

Only after defining your different personas accurately, you can then begin to create your own internal user activation benchmarks for each.

Create branched user experiences leading to Key Activation Points Only.

I know I harp on about it all the time - you can't have a traditional product tour and expect your users to activate.

Showing them how to do STEP 3 before they've even taken STEP 1 is a surefire way to overwhelm them. The following screenshot from an email marketing tool is a case in point:

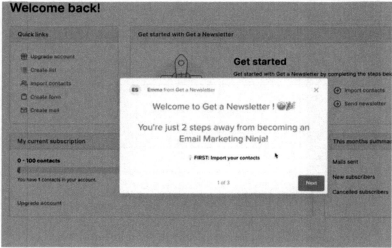

Source: Get a Newsletter

Instead of a product tour that overwhelms your users, create an interactive walkthrough that will push the users to adopt the key activation points. Make sure that the goal of each step in your walkthrough is to get to a custom event - the activation event you want the user to achieve.

Only that way will you know if the particular experience has actually contributed to a higher activation rate.

See an example of an interactive walkthrough:

STEP 1: Urge the user to link a social media account with a series of tooltips:

STEP 2: Get the user to write and publish their first post:

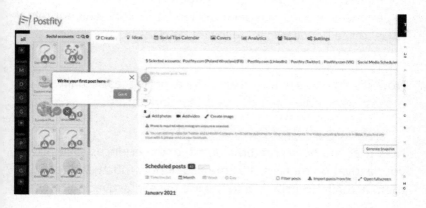

Now, the interesting part comes in between: In order to see STEP 2, the user needs to have completed STEP 1. We know what the user has done/has not done by checking which custom event has happened and which has not.

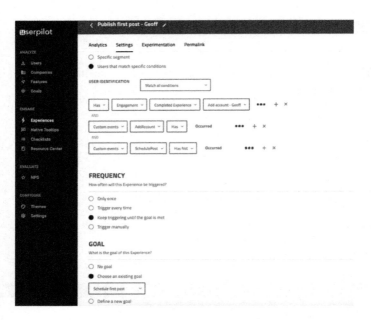

That way, you can effectively measure how many people
completed each of the key activation events. All the
experiences above have been built in Userpilot - why not talk
to us to see how you can build similar ones in your product?

Now, it's time to see if tweaking the experiences actually
moves the needle. Measure, A/B test and iterate.

Now that you have created a bunch of experiences to improve
your activation metrics, it's time to see how much each of
them actually contributed to the increase in activation rates.

The easiest way to do it is by A/B testing your experiences
against the null hypothesis or split testing the different
versions against each other.

Userpilot allows you to do that by simply ticking this option in the experimentation part of the exercise settings:

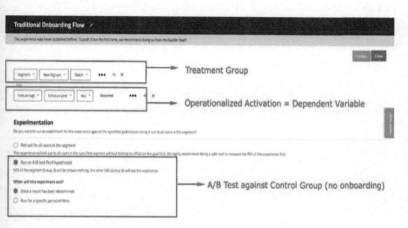

And that's it!

Exercises

EXERCISE 1: What is your key activation point? I.e. if you asked your users the following question: "When did you first feel you got value from {Your Product}?" - how would they respond? Or maybe you'd get different activation points for different user segments?

Note down your activation point(s) below:
Example: Activation Point for Userpilot: 1. Publishing the first onboarding flow

1. ....
2. ....
3. ....

EXERCISE 2: When does this activation point happen for your users (time since signup)? What steps do they need to take to reach it? What are the potential roadblocks (risks) that can stop them from reaching their activation point(s)?

The activation point happens for my users when...To reach the activation point, they need to take the following steps:

1. ....
2. ....
3. ....

Here are the potential roadblocks on their way to activation:

1. ....
2. ....
3. ....

EXERCISE 3: What kind of in-app experiences could you create to help your users get over the roadblocks?

1. ....
....
2. ....
....
3. ....
....

USER ONBOARDING
Definition

User onboarding is the process of continuously guiding your users across the user journey, helping them experience repeated value from your product, and getting their job done in the most frictionless way possible.

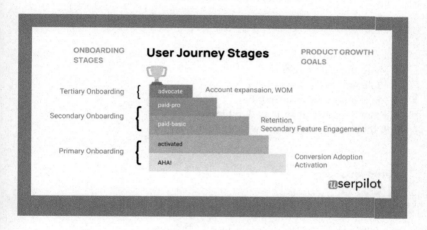

Successful onboarding is about showcasing your product's value proposition and helping users experience it too, by using in-app messages and UI patterns that shorten the learning curve.

If you're looking to improve product experience, you need to start with this.

A lil' party never killed nobody

I saw this great post by Ramli John, Managing Director at ProductLed, on LinkedIn recently:

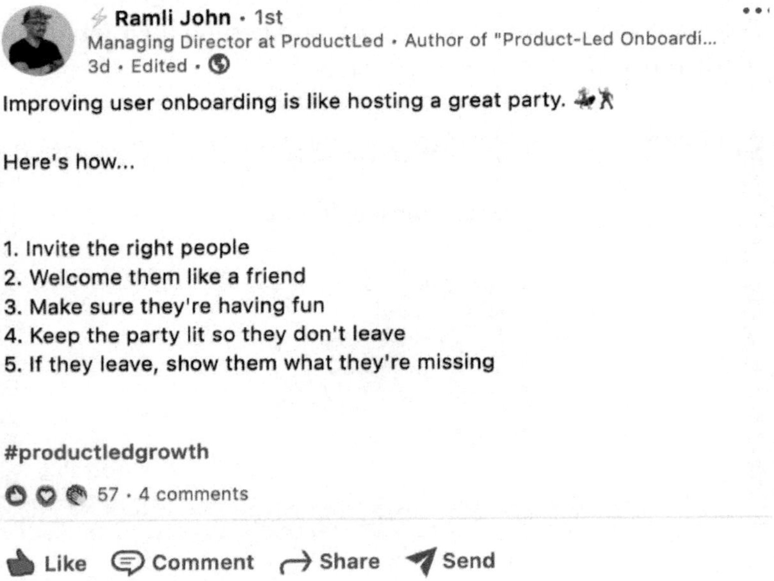

Ramli John · 1st
Managing Director at ProductLed · Author of "Product-Led Onboardi...
3d · Edited ·

Improving user onboarding is like hosting a great party.

Here's how...

1. Invite the right people
2. Welcome them like a friend
3. Make sure they're having fun
4. Keep the party lit so they don't leave
5. If they leave, show them what they're missing

#productledgrowth

57 · 4 comments

Like Comment Share Send

What a cool analogy! At first, it seemed like there'd be nothing to add...but the post got me Ramli-nating...

and I reached a conclusion that there's actually SO much to it!

Let's put our party hats on and imagine the scenario:

- Your guests arrive. You say hello, and then huddle them all together.

- You show them around the house. Room after room after room.

- In each room, you keep plopping more food onto their plates.

- You don't care if they've even eaten the last portion. You don't care if they're saying they've had enough and just want to chill. You don't care if they're allergic to shrimp! (Oh I've actually been to a wedding like that. The waiters just kept serving food...I had like five dinners that night.)

- At this point, some of your friends get bored and offended, so they are trying to leave.

- You block the door and to those few that manage to leave anyway, you send a passive-aggressive text making them feel stupid for missing out on such a great party.

Sounds horrible and ridiculous, right?

But as I've said before - we actually do a lot of things in our product that we'd never do in real life.

Your onboarding party will turn into this "nightmare scenario" if you use linear, time-based product tours.

Just look at this example from Get a Newsletter:

I haven't uploaded my email list yet, but it's already asking me to create my first list, and then - immediately - to create my first newsletter. In theory, I have completed the product tour. In practice - I've done nothing, and learnt nothing. I'm not much better off than I was when I first started. In fact - I'm now mildly annoyed by this.

If they had created an interactive walkthrough where each step would have been triggered only when a custom event occurred (e.g. uploading emails > creating a list > creating a first newsletter) - this would be a different story.

So now you get why interactive walkthroughs > product tours?

Interactive walkthroughs = outcome-focused.
Product tours = output focused.

How much help is too much?

Less is more, avoid tooltip overload

I was walking near my house when I noticed a couple of construction workers putting up these 'Quiet please' notices on the walls:

I stopped and couldn't help but think 'Duuude. You don't need to cover the whole wall with them. One or two would do the trick. *Seven* just turned the wall into a yellow eye-sore, without actually increasing the effectiveness.'

This reminded me of the experience I've had with some SaaS tools. Seeing too many tooltips, and notifications, or being dragged on a lengthy proudct tour (that completely ignores what you need, want, and know already)!

This is not going to make your user happier, or more efficient at using your app. It can actually make them pretty frustrated.

Let's talk about some of our FAQs:
- How much handholding does a new user need?
- And how many tooltips are too many tooltips?
- How can you prevent the nasty 'tooltip overload'?

I think there's a common consensus that you do not want to:

1) Show notifications/experiences to people who **don't need to see them** (because, e.g. they are too early - or too far - in their user journey. Or because they have not performed a certain action that is a pre-condition for performing the one you want to notify them about).

2) Show notifications to users who **don't want to see them**:
a) because they have already seen them or performed the action; or
b) because they have seen them and actively dismissed them, indicating they are not interested in what you have to say. (Believe it or not, it happens. They're not your mum.)

To avoid these situations, DON'T:

- Use linear product tours with multiple experiences that are triggered all at once and time-based (e.g. shown to everyone who has just signed up) regardless of whether someone has actually completed any required steps.
- Use time-based experience triggering in general - users should trigger experiences based on custom events, i.e. actions that the user has actually performed. With Userpilot, you can trigger in-app experiences based on user actions in real-time.
- Fail to ask the user for their Jobs-To-Be-Done, and then only show one generic experience flow to all of them.

This is exactly why I tell people they shouldn't use Intercom product tours (unless they don't care about activation rates and want to annoy their users).

Don't get me wrong, Intercom is a great tool for in-app communication, but when it comes to onboarding experiences...the tool is really too basic.

As you can see - the only triggering conditions are purely demographic.

How do we know this new user has any contacts to upload at all?

Assuming they do have an email list to upload in the first place - which again, is a guess - don't you think it would make sense to wait until they have actually uploaded the email list (STEP 1) before you suggest to them (STEP 2) - how to create a newsletter?

Here's what you want to DO:
- Use branching logic for your in-app experiences (e.g. show experience B only to users who have seen experience A, *and* belong to the 'new user' segment. / Show experience B only to the users who have achieved the goal of experience A, *and* have signed up less than 30 days ago).
- Make sure your tooltips are triggered contextually (in the right place, at the right time).
- Make sure you exclude the audience who has already done what the experience is asking them to do (e.g. by showing the particular step only to users for whom a specific custom event has not occurred yet).

Let me wrap that up with an example: You want your users to complete two actions that are conditional - STEP 2 depends on completing STEP 1 (e.g. 1. Add an email list, 2. Create your first newsletter. OR: 1. Add your social media accounts 2. Schedule your first post).

Now, in order to trigger the 'Schedule your first post' tooltip to the right users only (the ones who completed step 1 - added their social media accounts) - you need to restrict the second experience only to the users that have added their accounts: (PS. You could do all of this in Userpilot!)

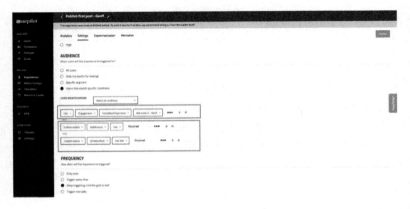

Atomic Habit-ing
Your User Onboarding

Atomic Habiting? Well, if you can Marie Kondo your closet, you can certainly James *Clear* your product adoption strategy. Honest confession: I used to be *very* goal-oriented. Think, visiting all the temples in Kyoto just because they were on the tourist map.

But most of the ambitious goals I set for myself - I either didn't achieve (and felt horrible for it) or did achieve but...the habit wouldn't stick long-term and I'd eventually revert back to my old ways (and feel even more horrible - my running times, I'm looking at you). And I kept doing it over and over again, until I read Atomic Habits. (I know, I know. Well, at least I didn't write "that book changed my life".) Promise it's super-relevant.

If you haven't read the book - here's the recap. According to James Clear - an atomic habit is a regular practice/routine that is a) small and easy to do b) is the source of incredible power:

1. If you want better results, then forget about setting goals. Focus on your systems instead.

2. The most effective way to change your habits is to focus not on what you want to achieve, but on whom you wish to become.

3. The Four Laws of Behavior Change are a simple set of rules we can use to build better habits. They are **(1) make it obvious, (2) make it attractive, (3) make it easy, and (4) make it satisfying**. The environment is the invisible hand that shapes human behavior.

Can you already see what I'm getting at? You can totally apply it to your work on product metrics. The only way to permanently improve your product metrics is to use the same principles that you would use to achieve any meaningful and permanent change in your life.

Sadly, very few product folks see it that way:

- they see onboarding as something they can set & forget.
- they focus on the features of their products, instead of the user's JTBD and whom the user will become after completing each milestone in their journey.
- they over-engineer things and make their product adoption experiences so hard to implement, then hardly ever revisit them after deployment.

Now, let's look at how we can flip the narrative and see how you can apply the principles from Atomic Habits to improving your product! **See your onboarding as an ongoing process, not a one-off exercise.**

Jeroen Corthout, founder and CEO of Salesflare, made a habit of improving their onboarding process by taking just one simple action every week. A small step - but in aggregate, it brought the Salesflare team huge compound interest.

How do you start seeing your onboarding as a continuous process? Well, it's going to get tricky - because while telling you that onboarding should be seen as a process rather than a goal, I will also tell you to...set a lot of goals to improve your onboarding.

But there are goals and there are goals:

1. Set goals for each experience and measure its completion at every step over time. Here are the goals Postfity (a social media scheduler) had set for the different features they want their users to adopt:

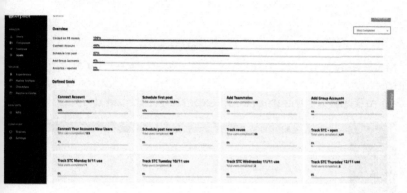

2. Time-block 'improving onboarding experiences - experiment' on your calendar. Every week, choose one aspect of your onboarding flow to improve. Focus on a particular stage of the user journey/ 'pirate metric' you want to improve, and operationalize it as the adoption of a particular feature (especially one that you can easily tag using 'feature tagging'.

Say I want to improve **new user activation** and reduce **time to first value**.

For me, that means more new users will become someone who can schedule their posts within their first web session. It will happen if they connect their social media accounts.

How can I marginally improve the onboarding experience by leading the new user to connect their accounts this week?

Make a hypothesis that 'changing experience A by adding a microvideo into it' will 'improve adoption of feature B'. Launch an A/B test for the improved experience to see the results.

3. Work on product adoption experiences throughout the user journey and product lifecycle.

If you're launching a new feature, think of how it will fit into the user journey and when is the right time to introduce it to your users. This goes far beyond a 'feature release'. Think about how to add it to your 'evergreen onboarding flow'.

4. Focus on the outcomes, not the features. The part when you're focusing on your users' "identity" rather than the features of your product is extremely important. Think about what they want to accomplish and who they want to become at each stage of the user journey. Then, think about what kind of in-app experience can facilitate that goal best.

In your microcopy (or microvideo!) focus on the benefits and the identity change of the user rather than the feature adoption. So instead of saying "connect your accounts to schedule posts to social media" say, "connect your accounts to automate post planning and save 8 hours per month!"

5. Make the whole process easy and rewarding for yourself (= know how to measure the ROI of your work). The third principle of atomic habits revolves around your environment. You need to make the desirable habits as easy and rewarding to perform as possible.

If, for example, you're trying to eat healthily/ lose weight, making it really easy for yourself to eat veg (by preparing healthy snacks) and very difficult to eat chocolate (by not buying it at all) is going to help.

Same with improving your product metrics. You want to make it easy and rewarding for yourself to even try.

Sadly, most product teams have to rely on their devs to implement any product adoption experiences for them... and the whole project can get so long and tedious that they'd rather settle for a lower activation score than bug their devs all the time.

Fortunately - if you go with Userpilot - we make it easy. You don't need to worry about involving your devs to implement any of the experiments or experiences mentioned here.

As for reward - you can literally set your goals for each experience, and then track how you're doing:

Besides that great feeling of hitting your goal, you will also have hard evidence of why your work on improving product metrics is important - in case anybody asks (and some execs tend to ask these questions).

This goes against everything you've heard from PLG experts

When to NOT invest in user onboarding

User onboarding can really make or break your product's success. But I would be an utter quack if I said it is *always* the case. (And oh, the words "always" and "never" should be banned from business conversations altogether.)

The truth is, you may be in a situation where you should just focus on other priorities.

When your house is on fire, you should run. Do not think about redecorating your bathroom. All the valuable hacks I'm sharing here that would help other companies grow exponentially could even tank your business...for the simple reason that there are problems that good user onboarding *won't* fix. And don't let anyone tell you otherwise.

Whatever situation you're in: community can also be a great PLG lever!

I snapped this quote by Dharmesh Shah, CTO at HubSpot today and thought I'd share it with you. Perfect timing too - it goes so well with our guest post on how to leverage your community to grow your SaaS by Natalie Luneva, author of a book on community led growth.

Dharmesh Shah in · Following
Founder and CTO at HubSpot
21h · 🌐

Product Led Growth is great.

What I'm excited about now is Community Led Growth.

Companies that create a massive community for their category and facilitate connections will win hearts, minds and market share.

Community is a catalyst for growth.

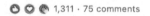 1,311 · 75 comments

 Celebrate   💬 Comment   ↗ Share   ✈ Send

And if you need help with your onboarding, you know who to call!

Your Users Will Not Get Enough of Your Product...

If you implement this onboarding strategy

Can you think of the last time a SaaS company really *delighted* you? Was it because of the features of its product? The UI? The website? Or maybe how the customer service went out of their way to help you outside their working hours? How easy was it to start using the product? The personal touch you felt throughout the onboarding process or how the company seemed to *exactly* get your pain?

Contrary to what you may have been told in your 'business' textbooks: emotions play a huge role not only in B2C sales but also in B2B. These 'little things' - how your entire company delights its users over and over again - ultimately translate into your Customer Engagement.

Defined as your overall relationship with your customer and the 'emotional connection' they have with your product, Customer Engagement seems like an elusive concept. Ironically - despite being elusive and hard to measure - it's also one of the strongest predictors of your Customer Experience.

And as Steve Jobs once famously said, to succeed: **"You have to start with the customer experience and work your way back towards the technology, not the other way around."**

So instead of thinking about what product managers can add to the roadmap, think about what the company as a whole should add to the experience to drive more *value*:

1. Show you really *get* your user's pain by personalizing their onboarding and making it super-relevant.

I know I throw the term 'personalization' around so much it may have lost some of its edge - but just think about it. If you don't learn what your user wants to achieve with your product and who they are, how are you supposed to help them effectively? Ask your users who they are and what they want to achieve right on the welcome screen (ideally, add a personalized video too!).

Then, segment them and provide personalized onboarding based on these answers:

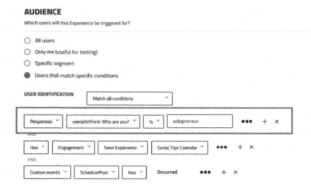

Get them to their goals ASAP. Don't waste time showing them around your product needlessly. It's about *them*, not you.

2. Once your user has activated and converted into a paying customer, don't forget about them. Unfortunately, many companies forget about their users as soon as they activate. Hence – a lot of users never discover the secondary (but no less valuable!) and advanced features of your product. These users never derive as much value from your product as they could. This leads to lower customer engagement over time and, ultimately – higher churn. How to prevent that?

Ensure you take care of your users at every stage of their user journey, not only at new user onboarding! Add secondary onboarding experiences to increase the adoption of advanced features.

3. Gamify the 'boring stuff' and use a sense of humor to build brand affinity. If you want to *really* engage, you can't be afraid of being polarizing. Show you *get* your user by sharing inside jokes related to their common struggles. Small changes like breathing some personality into your app microcopy go a long way in building Customer Engagement. E.g. look at this web notification: some people will hate it, but the ones that love it will be turned into StayFocusd hardcore fans:

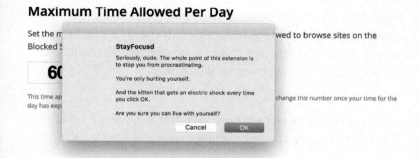

4. Make sure all your departments are on the same page when dealing with your customers. We call this Customer Engagement Strategy 'omnichannel' because the level of service can't break at any point.

You need to provide the same quality, tone of voice etc., regardless of the communication channel.

Having a great product experience with fun and super-relevant onboarding flows won't help if the emails your users receive from Customer Success are boring, disengaged or downright rude.

5. Overdeliver on the support & success. If the average response time in your industry is 10 minutes, shave it down to 5. Do something out of the box. Send them a gift for their birthday. Go out of your way to delight your users. E.g. Hotjar once sent me a free T-Shirt because I mentioned them in my blog post. It was super cute. I still wear that T-shirt. And I still use Hotjar.

6. Make a 'Cult'. No, not another Slack community or another boring Facebook group. A cult. A group of rabid fans who would fight for your product with greater chivalry than a medieval knight. A place for your customers to build real connections and feel like they are on 'the inside track.' Like they are part of something really cool.

Roam Research, a note-taking tool that is having a go at Evernote, is currently attempting that.

Of course, it takes the proverbial balls and a lot of flair to do it right. Will it work for Roam Research, or will it backfire? We're yet to see.

Being a try-hard at something that you don't really get or feel (the so-called faux-thenticity) is a huge turn-off. So figure out what *your* true voice is before starting your community.

7. Let the user take the spotlight. According to Nir Eyal, the author of 'Hooked: How to Build Habit-Forming Products' - people like sharing information about themselves so much, they would even pay for it. In other words: letting your users talk about their successes (with your product and in general) and then sharing their user-generated content, is a great way to increase Customer Engagement.

I have never heard a 'no' when I asked a user to give their opinion for an article insert, provide a testimonial for a website, or a case study for a blog. It's free publicity for them, and added value for us and other users. Seeing the ways other people are using our product can inspire them to explore more options.

To sum up:

- Delight with a personal touch to new user onboarding - use personalized videos and welcome screens and adapt the onboarding flow to the user's role and goal.

- Don't leave the customer to their own devices after they give you their money. Provide them with consistent support in-app and outside at every step of their user journey.

- Gamify the 'boring stuff' and use a sense of humor to build brand affinity.

- Provide a seamless and consistent experience across all channels.

- Overdeliver on the support & success front.

- Create a community that gives your customers a sense of exclusive belonging.

- Encourage user-generated content.

Onboarding the invited user

Have you ever been invited to a party and then, when you arrived, you didn't feel ***that*** invited at all?

Translating this into User Experience in the SaaS world:

- You've been invited to use an app by another user.
- You accept the invitation and end up joining a workspace in a tool you haven't used before.
- And then... there's no product walkthrough, no tooltips, nothing to give you a clue as to what to do next.

Let's face it: most companies don't do a great job onboarding the 'invited' user. And for some SaaS companies - such as collaboration or project management tools for teams - the invited user is the end-user of their software.

AKA - the lifeblood of the company.

In fact - most of the companies that have invited users don't onboard them at all. It's like saying to the team admin: 'Hey, this is your team member - you handle them yourself'!

Well, sorry - it's not your customers' job to onboard other customers to your software.

Even if they know them/ work with them.

Joe, our content writer - learnt this the hard way when he got invited to a chatbot-building tool:

When I finally manage to access one of the chatbots, I'm greeted with this:

Type caption (optional)

The chatbot is in the middle of being built, and now I'm here to help finish it off. Only, I have no idea how to use BotStar. I'm new here, remember?

Sounds **frustrating**, right?

Then, the second-biggest mistake SaaS companies make is... subjecting them to the same onboarding as a 'regular' user. But wait, **why should they get special treatment?** The referral invited user usually knows a little about the product from the user that referred them – so they don't need a full-blown onboarding. Or, the team member invited user may have different account permissions than the admin user - so if you 'recycle' your full onboarding flow, you may end up showing them features they have no access to or can't use.

So - how to onboard your invited users? Read our full guide here: **userpilot.com/blog/onboard-invited-users-saas/**

Secondary/Continuous Onboarding

Learn how to shift gears at every milestone of your user's journey

As you may have noticed - I love making real-life analogies. I also love driving. But my first driving lesson was a proper nightmare. I still remember how my instructor (a really blasé-looking, middle-aged man) walked me to the car, handed me the keys, and asked me to drive away. **Gas, clutch, shift!**

How many times do you think I stalled the car? **Hint: many**. But I eventually learned to listen to the engine, release the clutch slowly, and add gas at exactly the right moment. 12 years on, I'm doing it on autopilot.

And it doesn't take any extra effort to make the car go faster: when you hear the engine howl, you release gas, step on the clutch and shift gear. The engine disengages from the drive train, but it keeps going because of the energy stored in the flywheel. You change up a gear, release the clutch and step back on the gas.

Driving is much like delivering your user down the user journey. As your users move along the user journey, you really need to tune into them to see where exactly they are and if they are approaching a milestone: an 'AHA!' moment, activation point, conversion into paid user, becoming a power user and finally an advocate. **Each stage in the user journey requires you to apply a different user engagement strategy** - it's exactly like shifting gears.

It may be a little difficult at first but once you have nailed the conversion points/milestones when the user progresses from one stage to another, and learn which are the right measures both within and outside your product to push them to the next 'gear' - it will be like a flywheel.

In Rand Fishkin's words, when you build a flywheel "you put in the same amount of work (or less) each time and get more and more out of it the more you repeat it."

Now - the best, scalable way to this within your app is to:
- create the right user segments that your users will automatically 'fall into' when they approach a milestone in your app;
- create the right in-app experiences for each of these segments (corresponding to the stages in the user journey) to nurture your user, increase engagement, and help them derive more and more value from your product, and push them to the next stage in their user journey.

P.S. You can do both in Userpilot.
P.P.S. A lot of SaaS businesses are only using in-app experiences at the new-user onboarding stage. This is the equivalent of driving in first gear, and then putting it in neutral. Inefficient and dangerous. If you want to drive your user your journey properly, you need to leverage 'secondary' (and tertiary, etc.) onboarding as well.

How to apply the flywheel principle to your user journey?
Read the full guide here:
userpilot.com/blog/secondary-onboarding/

One paradigm shift in onboarding to improve all of your metrics

Onboarding never stops, you just have different goals at different stages of the user journey

Bookmark it, write it down, print it out. This one paradigm shift will change your entire perspective on onboarding, and will have a massive effect on your activation, adoption, retention rates, and even your revenue. **If you're ever 'done' with your onboarding, you're doing it wrong.**

Product folks who really own their product growth metrics know that they will never be done. Because onboarding - meaning 'new user onboarding' - is just a tiny fraction of your user experience layer. To succeed at improving your user activation, adoption, engagement & retention - you need to think of your onboarding as the 1st step in a **'continuous user education loop'**:

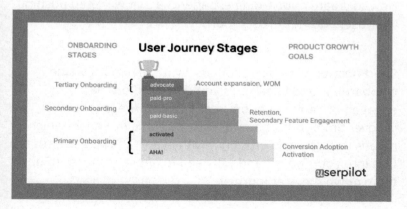

After your new user (Primary) onboarding, you should have Secondary, Tertiary & further onboarding. Each stage is tied to a different goal - and focuses on the adoption of different features.

In a nutshell:
- Your **Primary Onboarding's goal is to get your new users to the 'AHA!' moment** - get them to see and then experience the initial value of your product, adopt the key features (and only those!) and get them activated.
- Your Secondary Onboarding's goal is to get your users to **engage with secondary features** - this will help them get more value out of your product, and have more use cases. This stage will have a huge impact on your user engagement and retention. You can also use your secondary features as upsells or nudges for conversion.
- Last but not least: Tertiary Onboarding. You should still take care of your adopted and power-users. Those will drive word of mouth, but in order to keep them happy: you need to get them to use advanced features that show the ROI of your product. This is also an excellent time for **account expansion** - which will drive your revenue with upsells and cross-sells.

How to create onboarding experiences that will keep pushing your users down the user journey?

Short answer: with Userpilot! Start with Minimum Viable Onboarding, and tweak it as you go, based on the engagement and adoption rates you get. The great news is - over time, your onboarding turns into a flywheel - which means that you gain efficiency with every following user that falls into your funnel, and will need to apply less force to push them down the user journey.

Exercises

EXERCISE 1: What are the goals of your different audience segments?

User segment 1: Goals:

1. ....
2. ....
3. ....

User segment 2: Goals:

1. ....
2. ....
3. ....

User segment 3: Goals:

1. ....
2. ....
3. ....

EXERCISE 2: How is the user journey different depending on the different user segments?

EXERCISE 3: What are the discrete elements of your new user onboarding flows? When does the segmentation and personalization based on segments happen? What could be improved?

Elements of my onboarding flow in chronological order [highlight when segmentation + branching for personalization happens]

FEATURE ADOPTION
Definition

While product adoption lets you know how well users interact with your product, feature adoption gives a proper breakdown of what parts of your product are most successful and which you may need to let go of or work on.

Feature adoption is the act of your users adopting your product's feature(s) into use. Feature adoption metrics show you which parts of the product users value most. It gives a clear indication of how well your target audience values what you've created, and how it helps them achieve their Jobs-To-Be-Done.

If people are not using a feature it could mean they haven't found it or they aren't getting enough value from it.

In either case, you need an adoption strategy that focuses not only on feature discovery, but on collecting feedback and improving the feature altogether.

Knowing this information is how you reduce churn and increase retention rates.

userpilot.com/blog | Your Daily Source of Product Growth Tips

u

Killer features are like killer whales: Rare to spot and very dangerous

Don't fall into the 'build trap'

You know the story. You ship your product and you notice product adoption is, well...underwhelming. You go back to your team and start thinking. Are they missing something? And then you ask your users. You get a bunch of ideas. Your users are pulling you in all directions. And then you start building.

Welcome to the 'Build Trap'.

Most users don't know what they want. Or think they want something (and then wouldn't use it anyway). Also: when you ask your users what they want in an in-app survey or email, you will get responses from the top 1% of most active users. And they may have very different needs from the 'average user'.

As a result of trying to please everyone, you will dilute your product vision. Being completely user-led in your product design is the easiest way to do that.

Believing that adding the next feature will magically transform your product from an ugly duckling to a beautiful swan everyone loves is what I mean by 'The Next Feature Fallacy'.

Joshua Porter @bokardo · May 14, 2015   ···
The Next Feature Fallacy: the fallacy that the next feature you add will suddenly make people want to use the entire product.

💬 18   ↻ 789   ♡ 810   ⬆

The Next Feature Fallacy definition by Joshua Porter

This fallacy is perpetuated by the myth of the 'Killer Feature'. But more often than not, the 'Killer Feature' doesn't exist. There's only ever anecdotal evidence of its existence. In reality, sightings of 'Killer Features' (like killer whales…) are so rare that – when they do happen – they make the news.

The answer to your product adoption problems usually does not lie in 'having more features'. More often than not, it's about the more tedious, less sexy, and exciting problems of:

- **poor alignment of the existing product** with existing users: maybe you just don't have a product-market fit yet. Maybe you need to work more on product positioning and marketing.
- **poor UX**: maybe actually the features are there, but bad UX makes your product difficult and unpleasant to use.
- **poor activation and onboarding**: maybe your onboarding is leaky and people are not using your product because your time to value is forever.

And the **more features you build, the more maintenance problems you have**, the more complex and user-unfriendly your UX becomes, the more engineering power you need to build, fix and maintain your bloated features, and the fewer resources you have to work on product adoption: improving onboarding, feature adoption experiences, and retention.

This is exactly what the 'build trap' means. And it can be very costly. **So what should you do instead?**

#1 Shift focus from building features to Feature Adoption

"Building a bunch of "missing" features is unlikely to target the leakiest part of the user experience, which is in the onboarding." – Andrew Chen, General Partner at Andreessen Horowitz

First and foremost – you need to move away from the output mindset and into the outcome mindset. I know, I know – you got funding and hired a bunch of developers and product folks. Now you need to keep them busy. But being busy for the sake of it will not help you drive more value.

Shift resources from building new features to building product experiences to increase feature adoption by:

- experimenting and A/B testing different experiences (this can be done with Userpilot too).
- improving your new user onboarding to increase user activation rate.
- fixing any UX issues that cannot be side-stepped with in-app experiences.

#2 Invest in Evergreen Onboarding
Another important factor that affects the product feature death cycle is the lack of evergreen onboarding. By evergreen onboarding, I mean onboarding that happens at every step of the user journey, not only at the new user onboarding stage.

The User Journey

When you don't have onboarding experiences at later stages of the user journey, the new features you build don't get noticed after the feature release campaign ends.

This is also why feature death happens. You don't advertise your "new features" to the new users that joined after the "new feature" stops being new. (Shall we call it "feature ageism"?)

Instead, you could prevent a lot of feature death by implementing tooltips showcasing the feature at a specific point in the user journey, once the user reaches a certain milestone (in-app event):

Example: a secondary onboarding tooltip built with Userpilot.

This brings me to my last point...

#3 Invest in Product Marketing

PRODUCT MARKETING

1. Bring your product to market.

2. Promote your product.

3. Sell your product to customers.

Last but not least – you can prevent a lot of feature death by promoting your features more, and promoting the right patterns of usage to the right personas of your product, at the right stage in their user journey.

This is a Product Marketer's job and I can't overstate how important it is for your product adoption rate.

You need to keep selling the features of your product to your users all the time if you want to prevent feature death.

We got that whole 'user activation' thing wrong

Feature activation = key to product success

Ever built a great feature that...erm, hardly anyone used once you shipped it? (Be honest, no judgment from me - I built an entire product that hardly anyone used). What did you do to make sure the feature is activated? AKA: the user uses it, and experiences an 'AHA!' moment. The problem I see in a lot of SaaS businesses is that once they've built a feature, they just leave it there and hope the users will stumble upon it. Let's face the hard truth: most of them won't. Even if they requested the feature themselves.

Let's take a real-life analogy. Imagine you are working in a massive clothing store and a couple walks in, **will you**:

A) Do nothing. (You ignore the couple and hope they find what they want.)
B) Say hello, ask them what they are looking for, and then usher them to the right section. (Maybe even attempt to sell the new collection of summer dresses?)
C) Drag them around the entire store for 10 minutes on a pre-planned route?

You'd probably rule "C" out. In real life, you would never drag a potential customer around the store, showing them pants when they came for a summer dress. But a lot of SaaS businesses do this. See - that's the difference between a traditional product tour vs. an interactive, personalized walkthrough.

What about "A"? I know some of you will argue you like to explore on your own - whether at a store, or an app. But there's also a chance the couple would wander around, not find what they were looking for, get frustrated, and leave. Same happens when you do nothing to greet users.

User activation is one of the key Pirate Metrics determining product success. Do you really want to leave it to chance?

Now, I know I said user activation, not feature activation. But while I was researching some benchmarks, it struck me: we got this user activation thing wrong. Most SaaS companies look at new user activation as a one-off event.

Got to that first 'AHA!' moment? Understood how to use the app? Done! NEXT! Well, that's not how it works to keep your users long-term.

To retain your users, you need to consistently keep driving them to new 'AHA!' moments, and showing them more and more value. **Onboarding doesn't end with new user activation. It starts there.** You can have primary, secondary, tertiary onboarding... etc.

If we replaced the concept of user activation with feature activation, we would get a lot higher retention rates. Because then you need to actually think of how to make each segment of your users use all the relevant features and how to keep driving more and more value throughout their user journey.

84% of members *don't* have it

If you're one of them, that's a *huge* black hole in your Product Growth Strategy. **I'm talking about Product Adoption Strategy.**

Ok, now it's getting serious. Say 'Product Roadmap' and every product person knows what you mean. But Product Adoption Roadmap (or strategy) and you get people scratching their heads.

The poll I ran in our Product Marketing & Growth group speaks volumes:

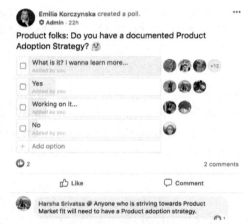

What?! 84% of the people who responded to the poll don't have a Product Adoption Strategy. That's insane. Why spend all this time and effort building your product and adding new amazing features if you don't have a consistent adoption strategy in place?

Meanwhile, your marketing department is probably spending a large proportion of its time building funnels, detecting dropouts and patching them. But hey, you're in a subscription business where most revenue comes from users' post-signup. Doesn't sound like rocket science that you should pay (at the very least) as much attention to adoption as you pay to acquisition.

You would expect every product team to have a documented Product Adoption Strategy. Unfortunately, that's usually not the case. As a Product Growth and Retention expert at Varicent, Aditi Gupta said to me recently in a private conversation:

"Product Adoption" is a huge hole that a lot of companies don't think about and have no "Adoption Roadmap" for.

Not having a Product Adoption Strategy for a product team is like not having a marketing strategy for a marketing team.

If you're just using a band-aid of product tours, **you're missing out on so many product growth goals**:

1. Increasing New User Activation
2. Increasing secondary Feature Engagement & Adoption
3. Increasing new feature adoption over time
4. Pushing more users down their user journey
5. Boosting Product Stickiness
6. Increasing User Retention
7. Preventing Churn
8. Achieving expansion revenue with upgrades

Oh of course you "don't need it!"
Trust me, you do

Guess how often I hear: "Sh we don't need onboarding. We are working on a really good UX"! Or: "We have Intercom." Intercom, with all due respect, is a support tool. And well, you will *really* need it if you don't provide any self-serve onboarding. If your new users can be bothered to write to you at all...

Let me tell you a little story. Last week I was trialing an outreach tool and I really liked it at first. The UI was simple. I created my first sequence with ease, scheduled it, and waited. And waited. And waited. **And I would have waited forever had I not pestered the CS via in-app chat** (about 5 times during the 7-day trial...) because what the product didn't tell me was that I needed to perform the first 2 steps of the sequence manually, go to another part of the application, and check them off there before the rest of the sequence would resume. I didn't know that. I, a new user, a complete beginner with no prior experience of such tools, would have no chance of knowing that. During our Intercom chat, they sent me this:

But of course, once I solved that problem - there were others. Finally, tired of the back-and-forth on Intercom chat - I called:

Me: This LinkedIn icon is so tiny - I simply didn't notice it.
Them: Oh you're not alone. Plenty of people have told me the same thing.
Me: You don't think a tooltip would have made sense there instead of having the users write to you every time?
Them: ...

This is what it *could* have looked like:

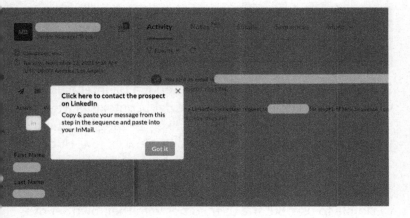

If you want to save your users and your support team some time, create in-app hints like this with Userpilot.

Now - this is what HubSpot does. The reactive popup from HubSpot you see below *just* appeared on my screen in Gmail after I sent a group email (I have HubSpot tracking enabled through my G-suite extension):

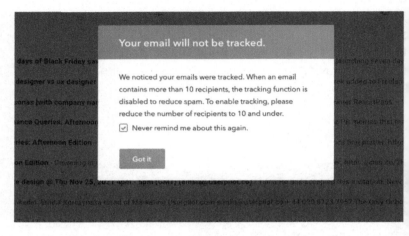

See what it did? It *informed* me about a UX interaction I wouldn't have known about, in the right contextual way, at the relevant time. Without this, I'd likely get angry that it didn't track my email and think it was a bug. Now I know, HubSpot.

Simple UI does *not* equal good UX. You can make the UI simple to use, but the user comes with their own set of expectations on how the product should interact with them. And, if your product doesn't do what users expect it to do - and you don't give your users a heads up on how it behaves - they will get angry.

So NO, a "really good UX" will not save you from implementing good *reactive* user onboarding. Even if you think "you don't need it".

Exercises

EXERCISE 1: What is your GTM process for launching new features? Write down all the steps. How many of them are in-app?

1. ....
2. ....
3. ....

EXERCISE 2: How do you introduce new features to your existing customers/users? What could be done better?

What I currently do to introduce new features to my customers:
1. ....
2. ....
3. ....

What I could do better:
1. ....
2. ....
3. ....

PRODUCT-LED GROWTH
Definition

Product-led growth (PLG) is a popular growth strategy that relies on the actual product experience to drive acquisition, activation, conversion, and retention. Customers don't have to book demos, download whitepapers, or speak with sales reps. They can just try the product for free.

Once users get value from the product through a free trial or freemium model, it's a lot easier for them to decide whether to upgrade to a paid plan.

The term product-led growth originally referred to self-service SaaS businesses in the 2010s. It was then hugely popularized by Wes Bush in his book Product-Led Growth.

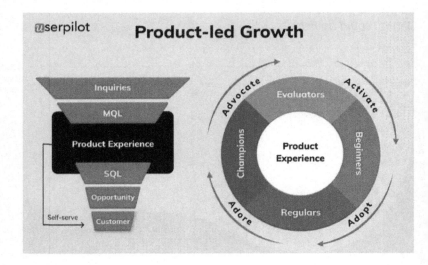

Toxic growth
Don't fall for it!

You know what happens when I go on Twitter and see that even Naval Ravikant woke up and chose violence?

Naval
@naval

You're doing sales because you failed at marketing.

You're doing marketing because you failed at product.

10:11 PM · Mar 20, 2022 · Twitter for iPhone

779 Retweets **290** Quote Tweets **6,474** Likes

Or when I escape to LinkedIn just to hear Jason Lemkin preach that if you're not experiencing exponential hypergrowth, you're basically dead in the water?

...I have a lot of pent-up Britney in my head: *don't you know that you're toxic?*

Jason M. Lemkin
SaaS Founder, Enthusiast & Investor

852 articles

A top SaaS VC to me the other day: "Once a SaaS business decelerates, it becomes almost hopeless. No one will buy you, fund you, or join you."

This VC certainly had a point. The good thing about SaaS is the revenue recurs. The bad news is it always has to be recurring by a materially higher absolute amount each quarter, each year. You can't go from $4m ARR one year to just $5m ARR the next and really get anywhere. You can't go from $15m ARR one year and then only $20m ARR the next and beat the competition. If this is the best you can do … then you're on a slow and painful march to irrelevance and atrophy. It also probably shows you've sort of fallen out of product-market fit. Cloud is so big today, that if you are past $1m-$2m ARR and have

No, they won't come if you build it. **And exponential growth is a myth.** I've recently realized that tech/SaaS influencers on Twitter and LinkedIn can be to SaaS founders what photoshopped Instagram influencers are to impressionable teenagers: an endless source of comparison, negativity and really bad decisions.

Off the top of my head: A friend of mine invested 5 figures in a SaaS startup that has now burnt through most of its pre-seed round. Instead of doing proper discovery and building the product in a lean way, the founder hired 36 people and now has built a product nobody wants. He has a 1% user activation rate and is desperate for more money that no one wants to give him now. Yet, somehow, he convinced the VCs to give him a pre-seed funding round.

Stories like that abound. Every day, you hear that yet another of your competitors has raised several million $ in series A. But if they scale it before they've nailed it, what you'll see next is that they spend the money on marketing recklessly, inflating their growth figures in an unsustainable way;

They spend on a product recklessly, building features nobody wants. If you're feeling inadequate because of what this or that SaaS/Product influencer has told you, here's a quantum of solace for you:

1) Exponential growth is a myth.

Re: *"You can't go from $4m ARR one year to just $5m ARR the next and really get anywhere. You can't go from $15m ARR one year and then only $20m ARR the next and beat the competition. If this is the best you can do ... then you're on a slow and painful march to irrelevance and atrophy."* Anna Holopanien's brilliant SaaS reads newsletter reminds me that well, hypergrowth is a myth. Growth *always* decelerates.

- Even the fastest-growing companies in history, like Facebook, don't grow exponentially (by multiples - e.g. by 10 in year 1, 100 in year 2, and 1000 in year 3). They still grow quadratically - by a steady value every year (e.g. by 10 in year 1, 20 in year 2, and 30 in year 3).
- That still means they grow more year-on-year, but they don't necessarily grow *faster* every year - if you've grown from 10 to 20 in year 1, that's a 100% increase. But if you've grown from 40 to 70 in year 3, that's "only" a 75% increase. Is it a "bad, you're dead in the water" growth curve according to VCs then?
- Now, where does the hyper-growth myth come from? Sometimes, these hyper-growth companies seem like they grow exponentially, but only because they either enter a new market with a new product, make an acquisition (or several), or their markets expand significantly.
- In finite markets, marketing-driven products follow an "elephant curve": "[campaigns] start flat when the new campaign is ineffective;

in the optimization phase, we test our way to incrementally better results; and finally, campaigns enter the phase of decline where the audience saturates (if the campaign ever flies, that is), the channel declines and in paid channels, the auction becomes uneconomical."

- The problem with the exponential growth myth perpetrated by VCs is that it leads many SaaS founders to feel like failures if they don't grow *faster* every year.

2) No, they won't come if you build it.

Talking to your users/potential users is free. (And as my high-school math teacher used to say: "free is not expensive!". If you're building new features so fast that you need 20 million to implement your product vision, you're probably not talking to your users enough to understand their problems. Apply Teresa Torres' continuous discovery framework and have some patience. **Lean and iterative product design is better**.

- I get that Naval probably meant well and wanted to tell you that no amount of sales or marketing is going to save you if your product is fundamentally bad (and if it is: see point one), but some people take that advice too literally. Before you fire your sales and marketing teams - remember that Word of Mouth is great, but it's not a channel you can control.
- Even the best product and UX won't defend itself once things get *complicated*. Some of your users will not discover features that they actually really need. **You need to keep marketing your product to your existing users, in-app.** The best UX and UI can't explain some server-level events that your user may not expect to happen (or not happen) when they navigate your product. You need to tell them what's happening behind the scenes.

So keep going. You're doing fine. That six-pack was photoshopped. That hypergrowth doesn't exist.

Want 7.2% more growth?
The best PLG hacks from SaaStock

Let's talk Product Led...Savings. Make your company more resilient with PLG. I know I know you're all busy congratulating Patrick Campbell on selling Profitwell to Paddle for $200 million... but I'm calling from Planet Earth where YC advisors are sending these emails to their portfolio startups:

Greetings YC Founders,

During this week we've done office hours with a large number of YC companies. They reached out to ask whether they should change their plans around spending, runway, hiring, and funding rounds based on the current state of public markets. What we've told them is that economic downturns often become huge opportunities for the founders who quickly change their mindset, plan ahead, and make sure their company survives.

Here are some thoughts to consider when making your plans:

1. No one cannot predict how bad the economy will get, but things don't look good.

2. The safe move is to plan for the worst. If the current situation is as bad as the last two economic downturns, the best way to prepare is to cut costs and extend your runway within the next 30 days. Your goal should be to get to Default Alive.

3. If you don't have the runway to reach default alive and your existing investors or new investors are willing to give you more money right now (even on the same terms as your last round) you should strongly consider taking it.

4. Regardless of your ability to fundraise, it's your responsibility to ensure your company will survive if you cannot raise money for the next 24 months.

5. Understand that the poor public market performance of tech companies significantly impacts VC investing. VCs will have a much harder time raising money and their LPs will expect more investment discipline.

   As a result, during economic downturns even the top tier VC funds with a lot of money slow down their deployment of capital (lesser funds often stop investing or die). This causes less competition between funds for deals which results in lower valuations, lower round sizes, and many fewer deals completed. In these situations, investors also reserve more capital to backstop their best performing companies, which further reduces the number of new financings.

   This slow down will have a disproportionate impact on international companies, asset heavy companies, low margin companies, hardtech, and other companies with high burn long time to revenue.

   Note that the numbers of meetings investors take don't decrease in proportion to the reduction in total investment. It's easy to be fooled into thinking a fund is actively investing when it is not.

6. For those of you who have started your company within the last 5 years, question what you believe to be the normal fundraising environment. Your fundraising experience was most likely not normal and future fundraises will be much more difficult.

7. If you are post Series A and pre-product market fit, don't expect another round to happen at all until you have obviously hit product market fit. The Series A Milestones we publish here might even turn out to be a bit too low.

8. If your plan is to raise money in the next 6-12 months, you might be raising at the peak of the downturn. Remember that your chances of success are extremely low even if your company is doing well. We recommend you change your plan.

9. Remember, that many of your competitors will not plan well, maintain high burn, and only figure out they are screwed when they try to raise their next round. You can often pick up significant market share in an economic downturn by just staying alive.

10. For more thoughts watch this video we've created: Save Your Startup during an Economic Downturn

Best,

YC

We talk about "Product-Led Growth" all the time, but considering that startups are laying people off in swarms now, and VCs are warning that capital is drying up, I think it's time we talked about "Product-Led Savings".

As the economy slows down, companies will need to be a lot more prudent in achieving growth. And anyway, our last Product Hero did the talking for me on LinkedIn:

Gonçalo Henriques ✅ · 1st   24m •••
Sr. Growth Product Manager | Advisor at FI0 | Reforge student | Ex...

PLG is all about costs saving

So here's how you can *save* tons of money in your company *and* achieve more growth with the PLG mindset:

1. Automate in-app onboarding and support for repeatable processes instead of throwing expensive Customer Success, Support, and Engineering resources on it.

I still see many companies skimping $300 per month on implementing an onboarding tool but then offering me to jump on 4-6 calls that could have been (easily) solved with a single tooltip. The unit economics of this doesn't add up.

What's the alternative?

I talked about Product-Led Onboarding in the last chapters, so in this one, I'd like to tell you a bit more about Happy Paths. You can't design great Product-Led Onboarding without knowing your users' Happy Paths.

Simply put - **the happy path is the error-free path users take to achieve the desired result**. You can represent it visually by creating Happy Flows. Conversely, if your user takes a detour and encounters friction on their path to achieving value from your product - they won't be happy.

To ensure your users don't wander off the right path, become unhappy and then exit the trail entirely, you should be using Product-Led Onboarding on the key milestones (places where your users can take the wrong turn!). Checklists and interactive walkthroughs will increase the chance of customers sticking to the happy path.

2. Improve retention and push for expansion revenue instead of throwing more marketing $ into a leaky bucket. Again - if your users step off the happy path and don't achieve their goals (ideally during the first-run experience - especially if you have a free trial!) - they will likely churn. No amount of new signups will fix that (especially if your CAC is high!) Whereas - if you increase your product usage by improving feature adoption with in-app experiences - you can drive expansion revenue and improve the LTV:CAC ratio.

3. Replace *extremely* expensive tools from *big brands* with newer, cost-effective contenders that don't lock you into multi-year six-figure contracts. Hey, that $55,500 annual Pendo contract you have is not a Louis Vuitton bag. It's not a status symbol. I see a lot of companies clinging to the choice they made several years ago when there weren't any good alternatives. Some of them are barely using the product. Don't cling to it like it's a life raft; the switching costs are minimal compared to the savings.

If that's the case for you - think about it. You could save $40,000 per year on a Product Growth tool alone! You can probably find similar cases across your entire department.

And what about your whole company? Saving $500,000 on expensive tools means you could hire five decent software engineers, great marketers, or great salespeople. You could spend that money *a lot* better.

4. Avoid employee bloat and dilution of responsibility.
I recently approached an engineer about a mission-critical bug on their company's signup page and he told me he's... not responsible for that page. He also didn't know who was responsible for that page.

Hiring more people does not equal more growth by default. It means you'll need to hire more management help. Some problems can't just be solved in less time by adding more people to the equation. And the more people in a company - the less personal accountability they feel.

You can prevent this "employee bloat" by automating processes or by using tools like Userpilot.

Conclusion? Savings can lead to growth.

I'm not talking about cutting corners here. Even in the enterprise sector - there's this false belief that if you're an enterprise software company and don't have a free trial/ freemium model, you can't be Product-Led. Fake news!

Your users (yes, even your enterprise-level, high-ACV, annual contract users!) don't want to jump on four onboarding calls. And even more support calls every time they encounter a UX issue. They don't want their work to be blocked because their end-users are in the Philippines, and your customer support is in Canada. Lack of in-app self-serve support is stopping them for the whole day.

So adding self-serve, product-led onboarding and support resources will improve your user satisfaction and *retention* even when you're sales-led.

In fact - dramatically reducing your costs of operations (especially customer support and success!) by making your products (including enterprise products!) more product-led - *is* a growth play.

SaaStr's growth secret inside

I went to SaaStr 2022 and there were a few insights that I really wanted to share with you:

First of all - I was wrong. At least according to Jason Lemkin - there's no recession! There's just market correction on the "unicorns" with insanely inflated valuations that had no roots in reality...or revenue.

Meanwhile, solid B2B SaaS companies (like Asana, see picture below) continued to grow like crazy.

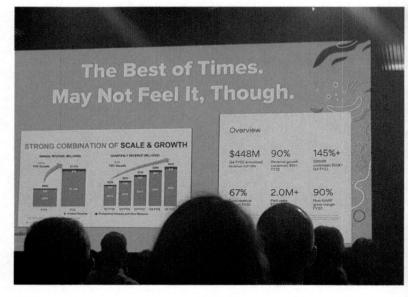

67% revenue growth, anyone?! So if you have some cash to spare this year, the best way to spending it is... drumroll...

There wasn't a *single* presentation that didn't mention this trend. Ok ok, I know - I'm repeating myself. You've been hearing it from me ad nauseam, but if you had come to SaaStr - you'd have heard it from everyone!

Three letters: **PLG.**

Now, let me explain why Product-Led Growth is more than just a catchphrase:

According to McKinsey (from November 2021), 65% of B2B Decision Makers prefer self-service, and 35% are willing to spend over $500k (!) via digital-self serve (up 27% from March to November 2021!!!). If 2/3 people are happy to swipe half a million dollars on their card now, what's your excuse for forcing people to "contact sales"?

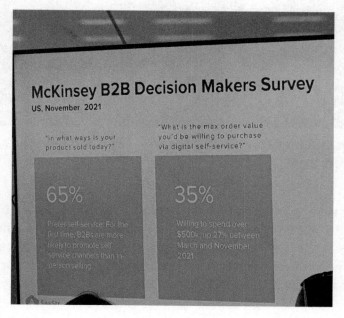

The Head of B2B SaaS EMEA at Meta also brought up the stunning growth in demand for self-serve product-led SaaS on Facebook and Instagram, vs. a flatline demand for sales-led software:

"But building Product-Led Experiences is difficult and expensive!"

Trust me - parties and exhibition booths with fancy swag bags are *A LOT* more expensive *and* difficult to execute. And yet - at SaaStr - I saw plenty of SaaS companies that did the former, but refused to create proper in-app onboarding or self-serve support experiences.

Call me a FOMO-monger - but these companies will miss out on huge growth potential.

And for no reason really - there are plenty of tools that allow you to execute your Product-Led Growth strategy *super* easily and without code. Tools like Userpilot cost a fraction of a single conference booth. Onboarding experiences have a significant and direct impact on user activation and retention - the ROI on spending $5000 per year on a tool like that vs. $15,000 on a conference booth is significantly higher. There's just no excuse for not implementing PLG now.

To sum up:

- SaaS onboarding funnels are a repeatable process or series of steps that takes people from entirely new customers to experienced users getting consistent value from your SaaS company.

- It's important to map and improve your conversion rate because it's the primary metric that tells you how successful your onboarding process is.

- Start with mapping the customer journey. Understand the end-to-end onboarding process, identify areas of friction, work out how to engineer 'AHA!' moments, and help drive activation for new customers.

- Next, analyze how your onboarding funnel is working. Define clear goals and how you'll measure progress (making sure to consider both quantitative data and customer setiment).

- Once you've built an understanding of the 'as-is', you can take steps to improve your onboarding and retention. Start by targeting areas of the flow with the most friction: can they be completely removed (or at least simplified)?

- Use in-app guidance to help convert users. Make sure you also give users the chance to solve their own problems: offering self-service support is a must in any onboarding process.

- Finally, you want to pick the right tools for the job. A whiteboard tool like Miro is great for mapping and understanding your customer journey.

- Userpilot is second to none for analyzing how your funnels are performing against goals and offering easy-to-deploy ways to improve the onboarding experience.

50% of our new revenue last month was purely product-led

Beat that, AE! Remember how 65% of B2B decision-makers prefer self-service? I don't want to contact your account executive to upgrade. So imagine my surprise when the-tool-I-constantly-rant-about made me do exactly that to add two more seats to our account. (They used to have self-serve upgrades, and now they've hidden them and made me send an email to sales. Guys. Please. If you're reading this - stop this now. If you want to flush money down the drain - give it to me.

Conversely - 50% of our revenue last month came from people just clicking the "upgrade" button and swiping their credit card, without ever talking to us. We made it incredibly easy for users to upgrade by showing an "upgrade slide-out" to high-intent accounts (you need to know which of your accounts are high intent or likely to buy first, of course - aka good segmentation rules).

So - wanna increase your self-serve upgrades too? First, you need to **close your Saas Consumer Gap first**. Simply put - the SaaS consumption gap is the difference between your entire product functionality, and what customers are using. It's not the same as the value gap - which is the difference between what your customers are expecting your product can do, and what it really can do. So no - it's not like your product is missing something. It's only your...product onboarding, customer success, or your product adoption strategy overall that's lacking.

This is, of course, kinda sad... (because building a good product takes so much time and resources, eh? So it's really frustrating when you build it, and then - nobody's using it. It's also probably a sign that you're product-centric rather than customer-centric.

So how do you fix this?

You need the correct data to identify your consumption gaps. First - you need to map your product features onto your user journey - by segment. What that means: each user segment follows a slightly different path of getting value from your product. Map that path for each segment.

Then plot which features lead to discovering value at which stage in the user journey.

Tag all the features on your map in your product. You can easily do it in Userpilot - you just select UI elements on your product visual, and tag them as a "feature" - then track their usage on the dashboard:

When you look at the dashboard, you can easily identify the features that are getting the fewest clicks. After identifying the neglected features, you can develop a strategy to reintroduce these features to relevant users:

- build a slideout to grab their attention, and attach the CTA button to a flow that will push them to explore this feature:

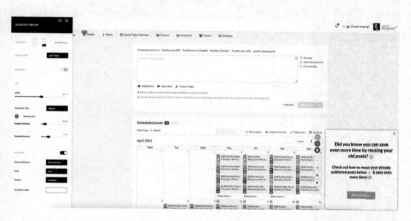

- put a hotspot next to a button leading to that feature to subtly push the users to discover them.

Etc....of course you can build these experiences easily in Userpilot, without code.

Identify accounts with the lowest consumption gap.

Now that you have mapped the user journeys by segment, plotted features along them, checked feature usage, and planted nudges to boost underused features: it is now time to milk the most successful accounts.

How?

Again - create a slide-out prompting your users to upgrade (as we did - see the GIF earlier), and target it to the audience that has adopted most or all of the value-driving features for the specific segment:

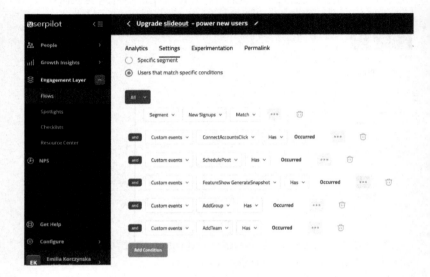

Now - these users will not only be most likely to upgrade - but they will also be most likely to be very successful customers when they do.

You're welcome. **Onto the exercises!**

Exercises

EXERCISE 1: Write down a few situations where you experienced Product-Led Growth in your company (= it was your product that drove sales).

1. ....
2. ....
3. ....

EXERCISE 2: What could you do to get more of that product-led growth?

....
....
....
....
....
....
....
....
....
....
....

EXPANSION REVENUE
Definition

Account expansion refers to the revenue growth of existing accounts.

The amount of additional revenue generated by your existing customers is calculated through expansion MRR, aka the portion of the total MRR of the company generated from existing accounts through upsells, cross-sells, or add-ons.

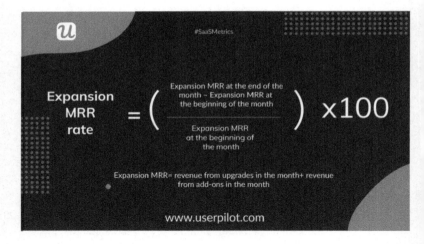

When your expansion MRR rate is higher than your churn rate, meaning you generate more additional revenue than you lose due to churn in a given period, this will ultimately increase the LTV and lead to negative churn.

"Pricing changes correlate with a higher ARPU"

One talk at SaaStr this past year that left me particularly captivated was Patrick Campbell and Allissa Chan's talk on SaaS pricing. In fact - some bits were so interesting, I can't not share them with you:

#1 Change your pricing frequently. Companies that change prices more often have a higher ARPU

Sorry for the photo quality - obviously, my hand was shaky with excitement.

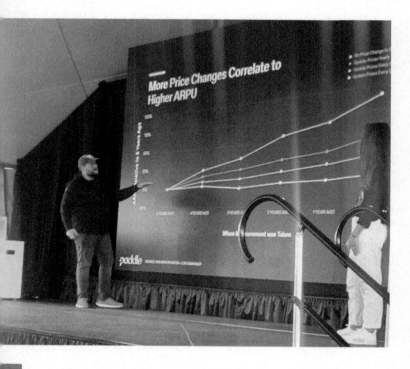

Why do pricing changes correlate with higher ARPU, you may ask?

- As your product changes, the value you provide for your customers (typically) increases over time. A higher price-change rate reflects both higher value-awareness, and higher rate of change.

Simply put: if you change your pricing often, it probably means you: add more features and innovate more > drive more value > which in turn allows you to justify higher pricing.

- It also reflects a general 'experimentation mindset' - if your team is looking for the ideal price point.

- Increasing pricing regularly means that you're going upmarket - you're attracting larger customers, increasing your ACV (while not necessarily increasing your user base as fast as you would if you stayed at a low price point). This explains higher ARPU per user. Companies should naturally go upmarket if they build more valuable and more complex products and add features that cater to large enterprises (e.g. SSO, team management etc.).

If you don't increase your prices, you're leaving money on the table. I feel we are guilty of this (ekhm...just checking if my boss is reading this).

#2 Localize your pricing. Different countries have different Willingness To Pay (WTP)

Did you know that prospects in the UK are likely to buy your product at a 17.6% higher price than those in the US? I didn't (and perhaps the fact that I'm from Eastern Europe, which is willing to spend 8% less on your product, explains it). Scandinavia is willing to pay 27% more for your product than the Americans (if you've ever been to Norway, you know why...). So **by keeping the price the same for everyone, you're leaving money on the table in two ways**:

- you're underpricing for prospects from higher WTP countries thus leaving money they are willing to payon the table.
- you're overpricing for the prospects from lower WTP countries, thus losing potential customers.

#3 Don't 'grandfather' your users on legacy pricing

This is a controversial one. You can't just increase your price and hope for the best. You need to get your customers' buy in. Look at the email **template Patrick sends them:**

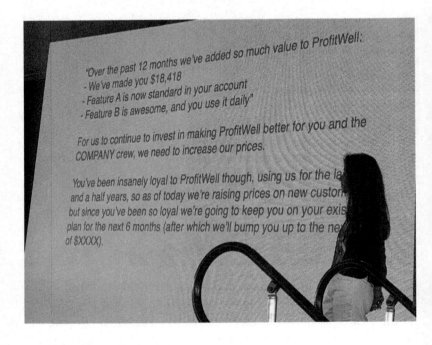

"Over the past 12 months we've added so much value to ProfitWell:
- We've made you $18,418
- Feature A is now standard in your account
- Feature B is awesome, and you use it daily"

For us to continue to invest in making ProfitWell better for you and the COMPANY crew, we need to increase our prices.

You've been insanely loyal to ProfitWell though, using us for the la[st] and a half years, so as of today we're raising prices on new custom[ers] but since you've been so loyal we're going to keep you on your exis[ting] plan for the next 6 months (after which we'll bump you up to the ne[w rate] of $XXXX).

He also adds a P.S., which admittedly - gives the whole thing a different, more human dimension:

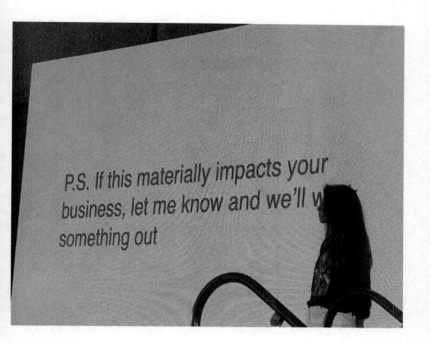

Now, I'd say - this email is cool and the P.S. is cooler, but you know what's the coolest?

This different idea how you could sell that, actually.

"The drug dealer method"

Instead of launching new features and then increasing prices for everyone, you could also try to generate expansion revenue from the new extra value you've added.

Here's how.

- Announce new features/ UX improvements in-app:

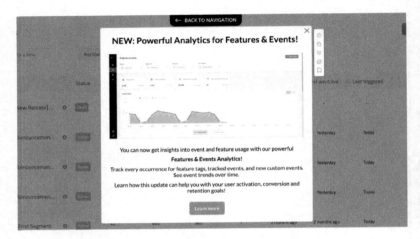

- Limit the usage of these value-driving features significantly or make them available to your users for just a short period of time - giving them a taste of all the goodness (and ideally, the ROI).

- Ask them to upgrade to enjoy a full version of the feature or to continue using it, for a limited time:

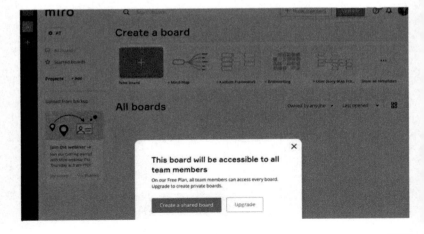

userpilot.com/blog | Your Daily Source of Product Growth Tips

For extra FOMO, add a countdown timer on the new feature pages, reminding your customers to upgrade.

Of course, you can create all the experiences shown on the left in Userpilot.

"What if we launch new features, and they don't upgrade?"

Well, I'd then ask myself: "Are we building the right features? Are they really driving more value for our customers?" Because if they are, then why wouldn't the customer pay for them?

I know not all features are equally valuable for all customer personas. But then why would you increase pricing for the customers that don't find value in these features?

If none (or very few) customers have actually upgraded after this play, it's a red flag for you that you may have fallen into the "Build Trap".

Engineering as marketing?
Or marketing as engineering?

Traditionally, marketers and engineers don't mix well. They see us marketers as these wishy-washy folks who say "it depends" way too often, and can't wait for AI to replace us. We see them as weird nerds in flannel shirts. But hear me out. The whole "us vs. them" divide is what may be holding you back from unlocking more Product-Led Growth channels.

(Product) Marketing as Engineering
This month, I met up for virtual coffee with one of the Product Rantz readers here - Gus Bartholomew, Head of Revenue & Ops at Grain. We talked about how we're achieving Product-Led Growth at Userpilot when I suddenly had an epiphany... Even at Userpilot, we delayed working on our product-led growth experiences, thinking 'we don't have the time' and 'it's too early for product marketing'. I hear the same stories all the time. But truth be told, you should never wait to build in-app experiences to push users to unlock more value from your product. You'd be leaving all these expansion revenue opportunities on the table.

And then, this just rolled off my tongue..."*Involving a product marketing manager in your release sprint, and baking the product adoption experiences into the sprint, would be a game changer.*" Duh. Why don't we do that? Why don't we make product marketing part of the engineering sprint? How much better would your product experience be if you planned how the new feature/UX improvement you're releasing should be discovered by different personas at each stage of their user journey? And then simply implemented a reactive onboarding experience for it?

Engineering as Marketing
Another way how engineering and marketing can work together to generate more Product-Led Growth, is by deploying free microapps as PQL (Product Qualified Lead) magnets. The microtools should be complementary and highly relevant to your core product or service. They should also be free to access and provide added value to your target audience.

One of the most well-known (and original) examples of engineering as marketing is HubSpot's Website Grader. It's a free tool that HubSpot launched in 2007 that scores your website based on factors like speed, SEO, mobile-friendliness, and security. The Website Grader intends to show users personalized recommendations on how to improve their site while weaving in HubSpot's products as a solution.

Userpilot also has a free online tool - a NPS calculator that makes it quick and easy to plug in your survey responses and find your NPS score.

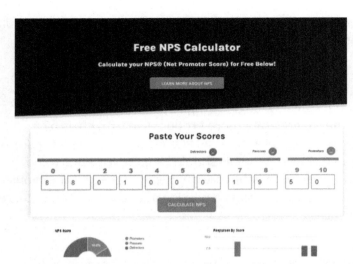

After getting your scores, if you want to use the data to segment your users, and send relevant in-app messages to those segments - you need to sign up for Userpilot.

If you don't have enough engineering resources to build microapps as marketing plays, then at least you can showcase how your tool works on your website, landing pages, and blog posts, with realistic animations and GIFs. It's time to involve your marketing in your engineering, or your engineering in your marketing!

How *NOT* to lose money and alienate customers

At the time of writing this particular chapter, it is #BlackFriday. It's the perfect season to...lose some money and alienate your customers. Let me explain.

A couple of weeks back, I had a great chat with Ireneusz Klimczak and Alexandra Kvasnevska from GetResponse. Alexandra said something that really stuck with me since. (And I knew I would be writing a post about it...).

"When your customers see these offers that are not available to them, they feel like they've overpaid, you're leaving them out, and they may become resentful."

Exactly.

Here's what most #SaaS companies do for Black Friday:

- Push heavily discounted plans for new clients
- Leave their existing clients out completely

Here's what happens as a result:

- You attract a ton of customers who are signing up for a very bad reason. They are price-sensitive, and ironically - tend to be a lot more demanding and create more hassle for your CSMs than people who made a value-based decision to buy your tool. And in the end: they churn more, bring you less revenue, and generate more support costs.
- Your existing customers are feeling resentful. If your tool is very transactional and you offer monthly plans, they may even cancel their existing subscription and sign up again at the promotional price.

Here's how you can do better:
I created a few examples of more sustainable sale offers you can promote to your users directly in-app to drive expansion revenue:
- Instead of offering discounts, add extra value to your plans
- e.g. access to premium features from higher plans in lower plans, add hours with a CSM, priority support etc.

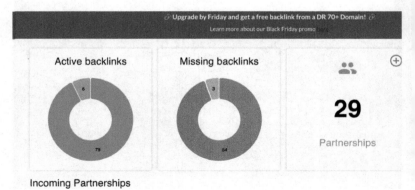

- Instead of only chasing new customers, provide special offers to existing customers to push for expansion revenue as well: e.g. provide a special offer on upgrades to higher plans (e.g. by giving extra allowance like in the example below if your pricing is usage-based) or upsell bundled add-ons:

With Userpilot, you can easily copy the slide-out and customize the text on for an audience of each plan, and then target the offer to the right audience in the audience settings:

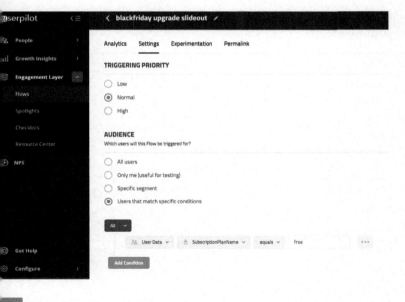

- Team up with another company (offering a complementary product/service to yours) to create a special reduced plan for both tools. You can then promote it in-app in both of your products, again, using audience targeting to exclude the users who are already your mutual customers with tools like e.g. Crossbeam.

Slideout being created in Userpilot

This way, you'll actually create more sustainable growth from your sales!

PRODUCT EXPERIENCE
Definition

Product experience is a subcategory within the overall user experience and refers to the overall sentiment and satisfaction a user has based on their experience with engaging with your product.

It's the thoughts and emotions that the users experience as a result of their interactions with the product. Those could be affected by a range of factors, such as the product's usefulness or usability.

For SaaS products, this includes everything that happens from the moment they first create an account, until they churn.

What's love got to do with it?

How often have you 'swiped left' on a product? How often was it 'love at first sight'?

I am probably a bit more patient and usually give the SaaS tools I'm testing a few 'dates' before I decide to dump them or move our relationship to the next level – but overall, my product experience is all that matters in the long run.

Let's face it - these days, we don't care how great a products' features are if it's slow, difficult to learn, or the key features are buried somewhere in the third menu and we simply don't get to experience the value (the 'AHA!' moment) fast enough. Welcome to the era of product-led growth.

A HISTORY OF SOFTWARE IN THREE ERAS

When you examine the history of the software industry with these drivers in mind, things quickly snap into three primary eras: the CIO Era, the Exec Era and the End User Era.

BUILD. Product-Led Growth. The End-User Era by HubSpot

We are – luckily as users, unluckily as SaaS owners – in the era of product-led growth. This means – the end-users product experience is what drives purchases; by word-of-mouth and instructions to the executives. Not marketing. Let alone sales.

The cushy times of selling expensive on-prem software to ICOs over steak brunches are gone with the wind, the competition is fierce, and the customers live in an almost perfect economy of abundant choice, easy comparison, and almost full information.

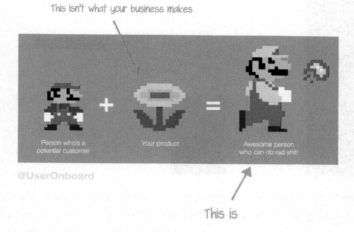

Source: The Elements of User Onboarding, Samuel Hulick

Hence, today, word of mouth is by far the most effective method of marketing. A Nielsen study found that "92% of consumers trust word of mouth over anything else (Nielson's Global Trust in Advertising report, 2012)".

What's more: "88% of UK customers will tell their friends about a positive brand experience they've had (Yonder Digital Group, 2017)".

So you want as many customer advocates as you can get. But on the flip side: 62% of customers say they share their bad experiences with others (Salesforce "State of the Connected Customer Report, 2018).

So, how do you make your product experience wow your users? Product experience is basically everything your user experiences when using your product.

From my perspective, a great product experience is all about (in line with the Valentine's theme) 'KISS-ing' at every stage of the customer journey – I mean, **keeping it simple** of course. And it's not only your product team that's responsible for that:

- **Make your signup flow really simple** – don't make new users confirm their email before they see your dashboard, don't make them fill in 10 fields, and maybe let them sign up via Google/FB. (responsibility of your product team)

- **Make sure your dashboard is clean** - use that empty state to highlight the key activation points they need to reach to see the value of your app – the 'AHA!' moment. (product team)

- **Use contextual onboarding** – trigger the right tooltips based on what I'm doing in your tool (or what I'm not doing... use your user analytics well) – don't drag me around your app by the hand for 5 minutes, showing me all the features I'm not interested in at the moment. And no, of course, I won't remember them ten minutes later because people learn by doing. (product team/ customer success)

- **Don't overpromise and underdeliver** – make sure the audience you're attracting with your marketing is aligned with your market positioning – if you don't have certain features that the industry leaders have and that everyone who's even a bit solution or product-aware takes for granted – don't target solution aware audience. (sales & marketing)

- **Listen and react (positively) to feedback** – don't use NPS as a vanity metric, actually record the feature requests and bug reports, and apply the right product fixes promptly – don't forget to notify the affected users (even if they had not reported the bug, but have been affected). Again, use your user behavior analytics to figure it out. (customer support)

If your SaaS product was a hotel, would it be a 5-star one?

Why do we pay so little attention to digital product experience cf. Real Life? Everyone's blabbing about how we are in the 'product-led era', how you should let the product do the talking, drive growth, and how 'product experience is King'. I'm not going to repeat the platitudes here (well, I just did, but let me fix that now).

I recently thought of good vs bad hotel experiences I have had and how it compares to my experience with digital products... **Think about it this way:** Imagine you run a Bed & Breakfast. A guest arrives. You don't say 'hello' to them when they arrive. Rude and weird, right? You don't ask them what they like or what is the purpose of their trip (Business? Leisure?). As a result, you serve them porridge for breakfast at 9 a.m. They hate porridge, are gluten-intolerant, and by the time you have served breakfast, they were already out. Oops, and oops again.

Besides the fact that the room looks like it was designed by your grandma's best friend 50 years ago, everything also doesn't work properly. **Last but not least: once the guest checks in, you go on break and never ask them how they are enjoying their stay**. Do you think your guest would come back to your hotel or recommend it to their friends after that kind of experience? It feels like product owners could learn a lot from hotel managers. The things that are so obvious when it comes to real-world experience rarely translate into digital product experience. So today, consider how you could make your product experience more like a stay in a 5-star hotel.

We ate our own dog food. This is what happened

The secret to almost zero churn & user love

Asking 'is it the best product' is like asking 'are they the best wife'.

As long as: a) your product consistently delivers value to your users;
b) you make it sticky, so leaving would incur a substantial time investment;
and unless c) you did something nasty and then really toasted marshmallows over that burnt bridge...

Your users won't be asking that question.

Think of your husband/wife. Are they the best husband/wife in the world? (Erm...if you respond 'no', I'm not gonna tell them...) Would you even ask yourself that question?!

1) If you simply love them => they are clearly consistently delivering value!), it won't occur to you to look for one you could 'love more'.
2) OK, that's a terrible metaphor, but if you have a house/ mortgage/ dog/ babies/ business together, they are 'sticky'. (Yes, I said that.)
You need to make your users love you too...and you need to make sure that they stick around because the alternative costs make it unattractive to leave.

Now - how did we make sure our product delivers consistent value...and is sticky?

We realized we need to eat our own dog food. **We built a Product Adoption Strategy for Userpilot - in Userpilot.** Now - building a single product tour doesn't make Userpilot sticky. That's the problem. New user onboarding is like 5% of what you can do with Userpilot. So if you do just that - you're not going to get the full value. Hence: those users that came and built just the new user onboarding with Userpilot were most likely to leave (and either does nothing afterwards or hard-code a sad, non-interactive product tour).

So our goal was to make sure our users:

- build more and more product experiences for every stage of their users' journey to improve their product adoption
- set goals and iterate their experiences to improve their feature engagement/adoption scores (aka run A/B tests)
- use our NPS surveys and build micro surveys to gauge their users' sentiment
- build a resource center to offer self-serve help right inside the app - where the users need it most...

If you've done all that, it's pretty much as if your product had a mortgage and a baby with Userpilot... We wanted more users to have that kind of relationship with us. This is also something you can do for your product - with Userpilot.

1) Create product experiences that help push your users down their User Journey.
Your users will only get more value out of your product if they keep getting more and more out of it. Attack the ROI-features of your product first - because if the user sees they can keep improving their Return On Investment, they will get hooked on doing so (#gamification), and will keep getting more and more value out of your product (smart, huh? Everybody wins).

Here's an example (Userpilot on Userpilot): if someone's success rate is 62.4%, we can nudge them to experiment to bump it up.

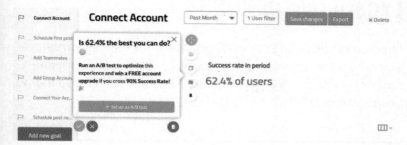

2) Pay extra attention to getting people to use the 'sticky' features. In our case - this is the resource center (as well as evergreen experience flows and experiments).

3) Cross-reference your NPS survey results with your users' in-app behavior to understand what kind of interactions in our app make a happy user...

Understanding the correlation between what users do in your app and how satisfied they are, allows you to help nudge users towards the behaviours that correlate with a high NPS. The results? Unbelievably low churn rate. We see our users doing the same thing with their users and winning every day.

Want more actionable Product Adoption Tactics? Visit: **userpilot.com/blog/actionable-product-adoption-tactics/**

Most PMs still don't get User Experience in 2023

I had an enlightening conversation with our CEO, at some point, he said: *"Page changes shouldn't exist. The flows shouldn't really exist either. We only added page changes because so many people wanted them."*

THIS. The "so many people" still think user onboarding is about slapping a product tour on top of your UI, to push your new users into every nook and cranny of the product in an 11-step product tour. It may sound very self-important now, but I feel we're a bit ahead of our time when it comes to how we see user onboarding. Heck, it's actually about the entire user experience, because **user onboarding never stops**.

The welcome flow is just 1% of what companies should be doing in-app to improve user experience and make their products really self-serve. The other 99% are the tiny reactive in-app experiences that help users when they need it, where they need it - without having to have any interactions with sales, support or customer success at all. Continuous Onboarding is the secret sauce.

But if most product people still want to have product tours... hey, we have to make some monies while we're waiting for the mindset shift to product-led to happen...So should we give up or should we just keep chasing pavements? Cue: an early Adele song playing in the background. Well, I'm Team Chasing Pavements. Let me explain why.

Why should we approach User Experience this way? I hear these "sales objections" against embracing a truly Product-Led approach all the time:

- "We don't have a free trial, we are sales led."
- "We're working on making our UX perfect, so it will be self-explanatory"
- "We're targeting enterprise companies"
- "We don't have the resources to dedicate to build in-app experiences"
- "We'll build it in-house"

Whaaat?

- Oh, so if you don't have a free trial, you should not care about user experience? Sounds like a recipe for high churn. Plus, even big companies prefer a product-led approach. Do you mean you will be able to explain back-end events that are never going to be self-explanatory natively in-app? How? Cluttering your interface with microcopy in case somebody needs the explanation, vs responding to event triggers?
- You mean enterprise companies don't want to have a good user experience and be able to use your tool independently? I bet a marketing manager in a large company in Singapore just loves waiting 15 hours for your CSM in San Francisco to wake up and tell them that they should have put a comma, not a space, between the URLs they've added to the display settings of the popup they built in your tool, for the popup to display correctly.
- Wait, hold on. Not having any in-app onboarding experiences means you will be spending *a lot* more on customer support and success.
- Oh man, good luck. Atlassian spent 2 years and $3 million on building this in-house.
And so on, and so forth.

It will take some time for the market to really embrace the Product-Led mindset. This is good news - you can use it as an unfair advantage.

Be the one who will lead the change and you'll reap the benefits of higher activation, lower churn, and higher expansion revenue.

Because let's face it - the world is different now than just a few years ago:

- Most companies have embraced remote work, which means people work asynchronously and have huge time differences. "Jumping on calls" is not an option for a lot of people anymore - they need to be able to use your tool independently.

- People don't want to be jumping on calls anyway. Even execs at the most enterprise-y companies just want to upgrade on their own and be done with it. Nobody wants to wait for your sales team to rise and shine when they just need to buy an extra seat.

- Funding cuts mean VC-backed tech startups will be cutting support costs - and unfortunately, employment. If you can't hire an army of CSMs anymore - how will you solve the problem of all the support tickets coming your way, just because you haven't implemented any in-app guidance?

Hope this gives you some food for thought ;)

SELF-SERVE SUPPORT
Definition

The self-service support methodology focuses on giving users the tools necessary to serve some problems on their own without having to reach out to support agents. This often includes elements like knowledge bases, chatbots, and interactive walkthroughs.

Harvard Business Review actually found that 81% of users try to solve their software issues before seeking help, so putting the proper infrastructure in place to facilitate self-service is essential for scaling your SaaS growth and for improved customer experience.

And while implementing self-service customer support may seem like a lot of work, the benefits will make the effort well worth it in the long run. It does take time and effort to set everything up initially, but you'll be able to see a decrease in support tickets and support costs, as well as trial-to-paid conversion rates and generally improved customer experience.

While a great customer service team can work wonders for the user experience, they shouldn't be the first line of defense for every simple question. Why make your customers wait in a queue when they could find the answer to their query in just a few clicks instead? If you enable customers to solve their own problems, their overall experience is bound to improve.

Blahblahblahblahblahblahblahblah...

That's how your users see your "support" resources
Marketers have been warning me against long subject lines -
now look at what I did!

Why? Apparently, people don't read these days. Guess what -
your users are people too. (I know. Shocking). So - if they can't
read a SINGLE line of text in an email - do you think they read
your help docs? Right. So - they can't be bothered to read your
help docs. They can't be bothered to write to your support
when they have a problem (and what if they don't actually
have a problem, but just don't know what they don't know?).

What's left to support them along the user journey? NOTHING.

In about 90% of the tools I'm using/ testing - there's absolutely
nothing at all as reactive self-serve support in-app (chat
with your embattled support agent doesn't count).

Letting you in on a little secret: my first job ever was in a
support role. At PayPal. (Any ex-PayPalers here? I'm sure you
feel my pain.) I quit after 9 months. I was so exhausted every
day after responding to the same questions over and over and
over again, I couldn't even pick up a magazine after work. PSA
to all Product Managers that are not using in-app microcopy
and reactive onboarding "because you have help docs" - this
is cruel. You wouldn't want to inflict this torture of constant
copying and pasting on your neighbor's annoying dog, let
alone your colleagues for support.

Now that I've stressed enough how IMPORTANT it is to have reactive, self-serve support in-app - let's look at how to write in-app microcopy that your users will actually read.

Hint: not like your help docs.

Microcopy are the "tiny words" that guide your users through your signup process, product and provide context on features, etc. It can have a critical impact on your conversion rates, so you'd better take it seriously!

To write microcopy well, you need a deep understanding of your target audience.

- Use your brand voice consistently.
- Keep microcopy micro - i.e. short. No one wants to have their UI cluttered with a wall of text.
- Use a conversational tone of voice.
- Avoid using technical jargon.
- A/B test your microcopy to see which variants your users prefer.
- Good microcopy can reduce churn and increase expansion revenue by answering users before they even ask you a question.
- Want to test different microcopy inside your app and see if it can improve conversations? Let's talk.

And of course - if you don't have anything to put your microcopy into - get Userpilot. You can deploy these reative tooltips in seconds. No coding required.

The real cost of "This email could have been a tooltip"?

First, let's look at why we need Product-Led Savings in 2023 in particular. The numbers speak for themselves:

- 81,670 - number of employees laid-off in tech startups in 2022 so far (as of 26/09, source: layoffs.fyi)
- 27% less VC funding globally cf. 2021 (source: Crunchbase), - 15% fewer deals, - 16% exits
- 38% less VC funding in Europe cf. 2021 (Crunchbase)
- And S&P 500 is down more than 20%

As a result, a lot of startups struggle to raise another round and have to extend their runways quickly. Layoffs and budget cuts seems like obvious solutions, but then - how do you achieve growth goals? **"Product-Led Growth" can help you not only grow but also save & extend your runway.** You probably remember some of my "This email could have been a tooltip" rants when I publicly called out companies for dragging me on CS calls for issues that could have been solved with a single tooltip. Now, we'll reveal how much these situations really cost:

Ticket resolution costs by escalation level in the US (source: Informa Tech):

- Level 1 Ticket: $22
- Level 2 Ticket: $91
- Level 3 Ticket $195
- Field Support: $416
- Vendor Support: $1015

Now, resolving a ticket through customer self-service costs just $2! **$22 - 2 = $20 savings per ticket.**

Ticket metrics - direct one-to-one customer support

Customer Satisfaction	Tickets per Month	First Response Time	Tickets/Active Agent	% Tix 1 Touch
84%	777	24.2 hrs	294	83%

- **Customer Satisfaction** - overall customer satisfaction rating
- **Tickets per Month** - total volume of new tickets
- **First Response Time** - average time it takes to respond to a new ticket
- **Tickets per Agent** - number of tickets solved per active agent
- **% of Tickets in One Touch** - tickets are resolved in one human interaction

Source: Zendesk

It doesn't stop there. We asked 24 companies with 700 employees (on average) what kind of support tickets they get most often.

It turned out, nearly 70% of the frequently asked questions are... "How to use {a feature}". So totally "tooltipable"!

Now, let's do some maths: 0.7 x 777 x $20 = $10,878 potential savings per month, at least! From "just" implementing some reactive self-serve support! (Because of course, one tooltip won't fix all your issues...)

So how to (easily) achieve Product-Led savings in Support?

- Collect your support FAQs and map them on the user journey (when the users typically ask them)

- Build interactive walkthroughs and reactive tooltips attached contextually to the UI elements ("features") that your users typically struggle with. Set them to trigger at the right time (e.g. when your user hovers over them)

- Add them + your help docs + video tutorials to a searchable Resource Center inside your app, so the users can find answers to their questions whenever they need them:

One of our customers, **GrowthMentor, reduced their support ticket volume by - 83% after implementing a Resource Center (+ onboarding checklist).** Now, the direct cost of support tickets (total monthly helpdesk expenses/ number of support tickets) is what you can easily see. What you can't easily see is the additional impact this has on your customers [Source: Statista]:

- 84% of customers prefer the ability to solve most service issues on their own
- 35% of customers would rather clean a toilet than speak to the support team
- 88% of US consumers expect companies to have an online self-service support portal
- 47% of customers say an unknowledgeable agent or support representative will cause them to leave a brand
- 91% of customers would prefer to use a company's knowledge base over speaking to a customer support rep

Leaving you with some food for thought here.

Exercises

EXERCISE 1: What are the most common issues your users reach out to your Customer Support with?

1. ....
2. ....
3. ....

EXERCISE 2: How could these issues be resolved with self-serve support, e.g. reactive tooltips?

1. ....
2. ....
3. ....

EXERCISE 3: How many tickets do you get for each issue per month? Calculate the ROI on each tooltip: the average cost of resolving a customer issue (without escalation) is $22.

"I get" .....tickets x $ 22 = ... potentially saved when replaced with self-serve reactive support.

RETENTION & CHURN BUSTING

Definition

In SaaS, customer retention is the sum of all activities a business undertakes to keep its users and to make its existing customers more profitable. The results of that work are often reported in the percentage rate of customers retained over total customers for a given period of time:

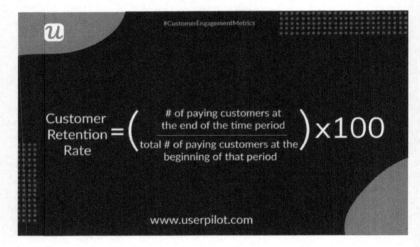

Directly related is the Customer Churn Rate (CCR), which is the flip side of the Customer Retention Rate. If one tells you how likely someone is to continue business with you, the other tells you how quickly you are losing customers. Measuring churn rate will allow you to plan for potential retention strategies. This is one of the most important PLG metrics! By understanding how and why customers are leaving, you can start creating more well-crafted product experiences that will boost your retention rate and reduce your churn rate.

There's only one reason why your customers churn

It recently struck me that...apart from chance events like your user falling under a bus, or closing down their business... there is only one reason behind all churn:

Your user didn't get enough value from your product.
Of course, depending on the stage in their user journey the reasons will be different:

- a new user will not get value because they couldn't figure it out (fast enough) - you failed at onboarding them;

- an activated user will not get enough value because after the initial 'AHA!' moment you didn't show them the other value points - aka - you failed at secondary onboarding;

- or your UX/ support/ pricing was not worth the value...

DRIVERS OF CHURN

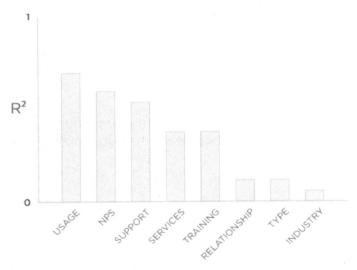

Source: glideconsultingllc.com/free-trials-users-arent-converting-customers/drivers-of-churn/

But ultimately, the bottom line is always the same: 'not enough value'.

Addressing the 'not enough value' issues at every point of your user's journey is what we call **retention marketing**.

(That's exactly what Userpilot was built for: to help you highlight the right features, to the right user, at the right time - and maximize user retention. And all without code.)

And because the whole point of running a SaaS business is to have recurring revenue - your job as a product marketer or product growth person is to make sure the user gets enough value to keep paying.

To stress how important retention is, let me leave that over-cited HBR quote here again: **5% increase in retention leads to a 25-95% increase in revenue**.

Just look at the chart below:

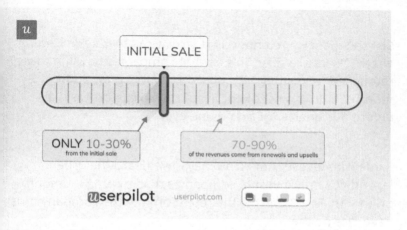

INITIAL SALE

ONLY 10-30%
from the initial sale

70-90%
of the revenues come from renewals and upsells

𝑢serpilot   userpilot.com

Now let's think about how you can create your retention marketing strategy and prevent churn rather than try to fix things when it already happened.

Because, you know, it's always too late to say sorry when your user has already churned. You can do a post-mortem, but you won't bring the person back from the dead.

Retention is not sexy?
What about negative cash flow?

Let me start this rant off with a question: **What is the metric that you like to track most?**

Growth, right? Acquisition? Lead velocity?

So - the thing is - retention isn't sexy. Growth is sexy. Getting *new* Users are sexy. This is what companies boast in these retouched case-study blog posts: 'How XYZ grew 300% in 7 months'. But 'How XYZ kept 5% more old customers than before this quarter'? Said no one ever.

Same with investments. You may have heard the urban legend VCs only invest in companies that grow 15%+ month-on-month. Ever heard of the retention rate the company must have? Me neither.

In the tech business world, retention is often the Cinderella of the pirate metrics. Don't get me wrong: growth isn't the ugly sister. It's really important. But chasing growth shouldn't come at the expense of retention: or it will come and bite you back.

Here's the ugly truth:

2% monthly churn rate means you need to replace around 22% of your revenue every year!

If your retention rate is low, and your marketing spend is high - there's a chance your LTV < CAC (your customer lifetime value is lower than your customer acquisition cost. That means you're actually losing money with every new customer you acquire)!

Even if you track retention, there's a good chance you're doing it wrong. User retention may be misrepresenting the data for you.

What we are all after at the end of the day is...revenue. So - if your retention rates are good in the lower-revenue-per-user group, but dismal in the best-paying customer segment: your average user retention rate will misrepresent the impact your churn in the different user segments has on revenue.

Duh. What's a product manager to do then?

1) Calculate your CAC and set retention targets to recoup it.

2) Segment, segment, segment! Which user segments have the biggest impact on your revenue? Which are plagued most by churn and how could you address it?

3) Address it - for the most profitable and most at-risk user segments first.

How to address it? Read about our 10 actionable ways to increase user value and boost retention:

userpilot.com/blog/importance-of-customer-retention

30% churn reduction with NPS?

It's not about the score, it's about what you do with it

One of our Product Growth and Retention group members, Andrea Saez, recently wrote a comment in the group: "NPS has absolutely no value", and referred me to her earlier Tweet:

Now: Yes, NPS alone is a vanity metric. It's not actionable. But it's not about the score, it's about what you do with it.

For example: Christian Sculthorp of Agency Analytics managed to cut churn by 30% in his company when he started acting upon their NPS survey data.The problem a lot of companies have is that they don't act upon their NPS scores because they don't know how to. And this is exactly what I wanted to attack in this chapter:

How to act upon your NPS, and what tools to use to do it effectively and at scale.

First of all, there are two things you need to do to ensure your NPS gives you more than just bragging rights:

1) Collect your NPS inside your app for granular and contextual data & follow-up immediately

To get results easily, you should conduct your NPS survey inside your app. I know some folks are hardcore email fans but...hear me out. Inside your product, you can be absolutely precise about when a user is presented with a survey. This enables your NPS tools to collect information that is infinitely more contextual than is possible with other channels.

This can give you an insight into how users feel about e.g. a specific (new) feature of your product, right after they have used it. Not three or 30 days later. Can you even remember what you ate three days ago? This will not only help you collect more accurate feedback, but also follow up with the right in-app actions immediately.

If a user is unhappy with a feature and gives you more qualitative responses in a follow-up microsurvey (e.g. 'it was too difficult to use') - you can automatically trigger an experience that will help them wrap their head around the feature, or give them an opportunity to contact your customer success team straight away.

This is something one of our clients - the social media scheduling service Postfity did:
- They noticed a group of users giving low NPS ratings.
- Then they spotted that these ratings correlated with the follow-up answer that suggested those users were too busy to come up with content ideas.

- Using Userpilot, they created a tooltip triggered by low-scoring users to highlight their Social Tips Calendar of content inspiration.

Postfity also targeted users who have not discovered this feature and are not using the tool to post regularly - to make sure the Postfity team can 'catch them before they fall' - and become the detractors.

So, as you can see - with the right tools - you can use your NPS data itself to improve user experiences. This approach will reduce frustration and increase value from your secondary/ new features straight away.

2) Cross-Reference Your NPS Score with Behavioural Analytics & Respond Accordingly

Cross-reference NPS scores with what users do and don't do inside your product - and **look for patterns**. Is there something most promoters do, that the detractors don't? Do the detractors and promoters use core/secondary/ tertiary features in the same ways? Are there use case differences? Recognize the behavior patterns that will lead to low NPS - and respond with the right experiences (proactive onboarding) before it's too late. This, of course, will lead to more promoters over time and higher retention.

3) Choose the right NPS tool

As you now probably realize, the best NPS tool (*ahem* Userpilot) that will allow you to actually act upon your survey will have the following features:

- opportunity to serve the survey in-app, and to serve it only to a specific segment of users (e.g. those that interacted with a specific page or feature)
- option to follow up on the NPS scores with a microsurvey:

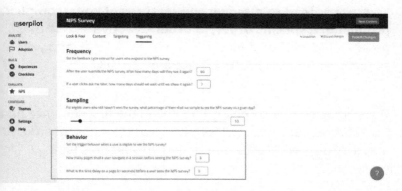

- option to cross-reference the NPS scores with other behavioral analytics (or at least to integrate with your user analytics tool)
- opportunity to create in-app experiences that would both respond to your users' NPS score (reactive experiences) and to behavior patterns that correlate with low/ high NPS scores (reactive experiences):

Ordnung muss sein

The order users discover your features matters, especially for your Churn Rate

"If a new user first discovers this feature first, they are several times more likely to churn." I heard that somewhere recently and it really made me think...Ordnung muss sein.

Your **users need to discover the features of your (complex) product in a specific order, in order to activate**. And that order may be different for each persona/use case. And yet - so many companies practice "onboarding YOLO".

Now - imagine that company I quoted in the first sentence had this feature that correlated with churn as their dashboard and that they discovered that correlation only months later...

Tragedy + Time = Comedy, right? But why wing it when you can map it?

Result? Many users churn/ never convert from trial-to-paid even if they were the perfect user persona - because you didn't take them on the shortest path to value, you showed them the wrong features first, and you burnt them with your product in their first-run experience. And if you burn your user with your product (beta), you may just as well kiss them goodbye. I had that experience myself.

7 years. This is how long it took me to return to Asana after I

"churned" from their trial for the first time. I hated the tool back in 2012. Now I want to 'Asana' my whole life. But still - I could have still been using it years earlier.

Convincing that user that "you've changed" is super-hard. C'mon. It's B2B sales, not a rom-com. They don't have an emotional connection with you.

So, what's the solution?

1. Map out your new user journey

2. Tag the "milestone" features your users may interact with on their journey

3. Create user segments based on the order of these interactions

4. Monitor the user cohorts' behavior based on the segments - does one segment seem a lot more engaged than another? Is one segment churning at a much higher rate?

In sum...order matters!

And you may need to intentionally walk your users through the features of your product in a specific order, perhaps even "hiding" or disabling certain features (rad, I know!) until they have adopted the ones they should adopt first based on your findings.

Wanna see how to do all of the above? Jump on a quick call with us and we'll show you how.

Exercises

EXERCISE 1: What are the most common churn triggers for your customers? What makes them think "I don't need {Your Product} anymore"?

1. ....
2. ....
3. ....

EXERCISE 2: When do these triggers happen?

1. ....
2. ....
3. ....

EXERCISE 3: What could you do to prevent your users from experiencing those triggers? What in-app experiences could you build to that end?

1. ....
2. ....
3. ....

CONCLUSION

Wow! You've gotten so far - congrats!

Hopefully, you're now more aware of the common PLG pitfalls that prevent so many SaaS companies from turning their product into a growth engine, and not a...user torturing device.

If you have any questions, feel free to drop me a line at emilia@userpilot.co!

Printed in Great Britain
by Amazon